The Bible & The Bench

Robert F. Simms

ALSO BY ROBERT SIMMS

CHRISTMAS REINSPECTED
Thoughts on the Real Christmas Story

THE EVANGELIST
A Story of John Mark

IT COMES FROM THE BIBLE
*Expressions in Modern English from
The King James Version of the Bible*

CHRISTIANITY MADE SIMPLE
The Message of Paul's Letter to the Romans

WALKING THE WALK,
NOT JUST TALKING THE TALK
A Commentary on James

WHERE DID I COME FROM
Your Spiritual Nature and What it Means to You

7 DAYS
*Seven-Day Waiting Periods in the Bible
And a Plan for Spiritual Renewal*

PONDER, PRAY, PRACTICE
366 Daily Devotions for Thinking Christians

SACRED SUBVERSION
*How Some Churches Defeat their Pastors
And Destroy Themselves*

To Judge Henry Mims,
who always treated me
as an equal, and still
calls me Judge.

The Bible & The Bench

Robert F. Simms

If not otherwise marked, scriptures are from the
King James Version of the Bible.

ISBN: 978-1-7378117-1-8
Published in the United States by
Robert F. Simms
Greer, South Carolina

CONTENTS

It's Personal for Me

The notion of the connection of the Bible to the role of a judge is very personal for me. I became a Christian at the age of seven. Midway through my college career I became dramatically convinced God wanted me to follow his calling to preach the gospel. I went to a seminary for a graduate degree, and while there I began serving the first of six churches as a full time pastor. I then became an interim pastor for three successive churches. But a number of years before I would be old enough to consider retiring, something quite different happened. I became a judge.

From an early age I had been aware of the legacy of the legal profession in my family. My paternal grandfather was a prominent lawyer in North Carolina whom some people, curiously, called "judge," though he never was one. Two of his sons joined him in his law firm as they graduated law school and passed the bar a few years apart. One of them ultimately argued a case before the U.S. Supreme Court. At family gatherings at "the old home place," as they called it by then, the lawyer sons occasionally suggested I might think about entering the legal profession someday.

When I went to Wake Forest University, where all of them had gone, I briefly considered law, but eventually went into Christian ministry, and would have continued in that path thirty some years later had it not been for an idea of a friend of mine, and, I am convinced, the intervention of God. The friend was a magistrate and Summary Court judge. The idea he had was that I might be

3

just the person to succeed him on his bench.

In South Carolina, Summary Court judges are appointed by the governor. The governor gets a nomination from the state senatorial delegation from the district where a vacancy on the bench occurs. The specific senator for that area brings his nomination to the delegation. In this case, my judge friend's senator asked him who he thought would make a good replacement for him.

The senator might have asked the question of his judge anyway, but in this case the judge had served as a magistrate and Summary Court judge for our county and my township for thirty-nine years. The law required him to retire in the year he turned seventy-two. He was an institution, highly respected in the state, but he had to hang up his robe.

He called me. He indicated that he had called no one else. When asked by his senator who he thought would make a good replacement for him on the bench, he thought of me right away.

The judge and I had been friends ever since 1961, when I was twelve and he was twenty-seven. Obviously he wasn't a friend like boys in my school. He was a young adult in my father's church and a soloist in the church choir. Next to my father's solo voice, which was incomparable, the judge's voice was a close runner-up, and I aspired to be as good as they were. Later on when I was off at college and then even farther away in seminary, on trips home I would make sure to speak to the judge, especially if he happened to sing one of his favorite solos that Sunday.

Whether because my father was the pastor of my hometown church or for some other reason, there were several older members, both men and women, who "took a liking" to me in a special way. A church woman about the judge's age who later became mayor of the city adopted me in a way, remembering my birthday year to year and giving me the occasional gift. A Brit who married during World War 2 and moved over to the States permanently seemed to favor me over the years. And my friend the judge who took the bench the year I graduated high school had

4

asked my dad about me through the years and kept up with my career in ministry, until one day he called me out of the blue and asked if I would like to be the man who replaced him on his bench.

It was a God-moment. I've had several God-moments in my life, career-directing times when the speaking, the moving, the inspiration of God was as clear as day and bright as sunshine. One of those moments was when God called me into full time Christian service to preach. Now decades later, God was using an occasional friend to open the door to my next assignment in his will.

I didn't stop preaching; in fact, it was my one question of the judge when he surprised me by asking if I'd like to succeed him. I wanted to know if there were any reason being a judge would preclude my preaching. I was serving as an interim pastor. He said no, and further, he said being a judge shouldn't keep me from teaching—I was an adjunct professor at a local university, in the Christian Studies department. When he gave me those responses, I was immediate in my answer, because I was profoundly certain in heart and mind: Yes!

The process of my becoming a judge, even at the level I would be entering, took a year. I had to demonstrate my qualifications even to be eligible; I had to pass the senator's personal test—an interview with him; I had to pass a battery of personality and cognitive tests; I had to submit certified copies of various documents including diplomas; I had to successfully complete preparatory courses in civil and criminal law; I had to complete court observations in various courts of the county; ultimately, I would have to move, because I was two hundred yards outside the senator's district; I interviewed with circuit court judges and the chief magistrate of the county; and I had to pass lengthy and rigorous exams proving my knowledge and competency to function as a magistrate and Summary Court judge. When my friend the judge called me, I was enrolled in doctoral studies for a teaching degree in Theology. My God-moment convinced me immediately to withdraw from the degree program and forge full speed ahead with preparation for the judiciary.

While I was doing my part, the senate and then the governor were doing their's, and in a year's time I held in my hands the letter of appointment. I was sworn in. The day before, I was a preacher. A day later, I was a judge. I was both, but my paying career had shifted. God had provided for me and my family before through his churches. Now, he was going to provide for us through the State.

I suppose the transition from preacher to judge does seem a bit curious. I wish I had twenty dollars (it used to be "a nickel", but there's been inflation!) for every person who asked me how I went from being in the ministry to being in the judiciary. Most of them have been new acquaintances who were simply curious, though one was an antagonist who wouldn't have thought I'd be fit to be a dog catcher—but I digress. I devised an answer to the question the first time it was asked. I said it wasn't such a leap; in fact, it was the best of both worlds: I got to preach the Book to them on Sunday and throw the book at them on Monday.

Privately, I marveled at the transition, myself. Earlier in life I would never have guessed God's plan would take me into judicial work. I went from wearing a white robe in the baptistry to wearing a black one on the bench. I went from signing marriage certificates to signing arrest warrants. I went from preaching salvation from judgment to uttering judgments myself. I did both, just on different days.

As a consequence of the curious admixture of the ministry and the magistracy in my life, I determined early in my thinking about the subject to write this book from a personal perspective, not merely an academic one. I wanted to record my experience of seeing how the written word of God informs and inspires the conduct of the judge. *The Bible & The Bench* is the result.

There was a time in the United States when most courts actually had a Bible on the bench. It was principally used in swearing in witnesses, who would put their left hands on the Bible and raise their right hands vowing to tell the truth, the whole truth, and nothing but the truth. Lately courts have become reluctant to require the use of anything other than the raised hand in swearing to tell the truth, and most have gone to offering the witness the option of swearing or simply affirming—an accommodation of those who for religious reasons say they don't swear to anything.

My not being one who subscribes to many token acts in the first place, it never seemed vital for a Bible to somehow guarantee a witness wouldn't lie. Besides, in today's climate, there would be calls by Muslims to swear on the Qur'an, and so on. I used the simple oath saying, "Do you solemnly swear or affirm that you will tell the truth, the whole truth, and nothing but the truth."

But there's something telling about the growing absence of the Bible on the bench in American courts. For sure, it does these things: it indicates the recognition that our country is not a theocracy; it suggests that people who believe the Bible cannot coerce people who don't, particularly, to honor it the way we do; and it comports with the guarantee of the First Amendment that we honor the rights of all to pursue whatever religion they like, or none at all. But at the same time, the erasure of the Bible from the picture is emblematic of the diminishing influence of Christianity on the United States.

A Gallup poll published in 2022 found that over the last ten years Americans answering "Yes" to the simple question, "Do you believe in God," went from 92% to 81%—an astonishing decrease. The figure in 1944 was 96%, and during the 1950s and 60s it was consistently 98%. This particular poll was of adults, but obviously those who were preteens in 2011 became adults by 2022, so the poll reflects the beliefs of a significant number of Gen Y and Gen Z young people.

This poll is disturbing to people of faith—the subject of perhaps another book—but it simply helps explain the deliberate secularization of some things in American culture, including the legal system, that were formerly painted with unapologetic, religious colors.

To be sure, however, there is an influence of the Bible in American law that wouldn't be easily erased. The American system of jurisprudence derives mostly from the English system as it existed in the mid 18th century, and backward through the systems of the Church of England, the Catholic Church, the Roman Empire, and even remotely that of the Greeks and the Egyptians. The Catholic Church's system, which merged with the Roman model after A.D. 325, was based in great part on the Biblical model.

But whatever the form of jurisprudence was or has become, wherever judges existed to determine cases between the state and a defendant, or between citizens themselves, the Bible stood as a spiritual guidebook for those judges. It showed them where their authority ultimately came from and gave them a holy charge to live justly and do justice to others.

The Bible & The Bench is not intended to be exhaustive, as should be self-evident from its short length. Instead, this little study looks at the whole Biblical record and boils down the outstanding passages that focus on God's message to judges, particularly as that message has made its impact on my own experience.

Principles of the Judiciary

Two plaques I made hung on the wall behind my chair in chambers for the years I served as a magistrate and Summary Court judge. They featured two sayings, portions of Bible verses about the idea of being a judge. One of them came from Genesis:

> **Far be it from you to do such a thing—to kill the righteous with the wicked, treating the righteous and the wicked alike. Far be it from you! Will not the Judge of all the earth do right?" (Genesis 18:25 NIV).**

The phrase on the plaque was the last part of this verse: Will not the Judge of all the earth do right? It was spoken by Abraham. He had been visited by three "men," as the Bible describes them. Two of the men were angels, as we come to see. The third, we can deduce from careful reading, was the LORD himself, appearing in what theologians variously call a theophany or a Christophy. The three appeared to Abraham and Sarah that day to tell them they would have a child, though they were both quite old, and to inform them of something else. The LORD said that Sodom was indescribably wicked, and that he was going down to destroy the city.

Abraham thought instantly of people in Sodom who were not wicked, namely his nephew Lot and his family. Why they were living in Sodom was anybody's guess, but they had not become immoral like the general population there. Lot was trying to maintain godly principles, against the powerful, pervasive and perverse influence of the rest of the city. So Abraham spoke up, asking if the LORD intended to kill the righteous along with the wicked. He had the boldness to speak about the LORD'S character to the LORD himself, challenging him on the principle of justice: was it right to treat the righteous and the wicked the same way?

Will not the Judge of all the earth do right?

Before the reader thinks of the age-old "problem of evil" that provides an excuse for many an atheist to ridicule Judaism and Christianity, note that the LORD'S answer returns the challenge to Abraham. While Abraham had generalized about the "righteous" people in Sodom, the LORD makes it clear their number was very small. Abraham asked if he would spare Sodom for fifty righteous. He would. How about for forty-five? He would. Down and down the number went, until the LORD agreed he would spare the entire city for only ten righteous people. But there weren't even that many. The LORD went down, had the angels lead Lot's family to a safe place miles away, and then the city was destroyed in some cataclysm from heaven that made the history books of the time and ever since.

This account in Genesis is ultimately a picture of the final judgment God will bring on the world. He will take the righteous out of the world and then destroy the vile and perverse place it will have become. There will be nothing unjust about God's judgment in that great future event, and there is nothing unjust about God's dealings with the world in the here and now.

What that encounter between the LORD and Abraham illustrates is that God is the ultimate source of perfect justice.

God, the Ultimate Source of Justice

The term "postmodernism" describes a philosophical movement that many people say largely replaced the "modern" philosophy characterizing the 17th through the 19th centuries. We didn't hear much about postmodernism in the general public until the core belief of the philosophy began to be expressed in successive generations of people who denied that there is any such thing as Truth. These days, for instance, many people insist that there's "my truth" or "your truth," but no such thing as a Truth that is apart from human opinion, a standard that doesn't depend on human reasoning or feelings for what it is.

Obviously, this kind of thinking denies the message of the Bible on the matter, which can be summarized in the statement that God's word is Truth, and that God epitomizes Truth. As a corollary to that proposition is the statement that God's law is the perfect standard of righteousness: what God says is right or wrong is always right or wrong, regardless of the date or the latitude and longitude. Moral law does not change with culture, social movements, national boundaries or leadership, or with the age in which human beings live.

Justice on a personal level means conformity to truth. A just person is one who lives according to the truths of God.

For a government to do justice means both that it operates justly with respect to the citizens, and also that through its system of jurisprudence it holds persons accountable for their actions according to the standard of law. The ultimate law is from the ultimate source of right and wrong: God. And he, as ultimate judge, is also perfectly just, so in his role as judge of all the earth, he will certainly do right.

Human governments are a reflection of God's rule in the higher sense. In fact, the Apostle Paul stated clearly that "there is no authority except that which God has established" (Romans 13:1 NIV). In this view, God is seen as the ultimate authority and earthly authorities, or governments, come to be because of the permission or sanction of God. This can be a difficult teaching, especially in light of some of the most oppressive governments history records. But Paul went on to say, "For the one in authority is God's servant for your good. But if you do wrong, be afraid, for rulers do not bear the sword for no reason. They are God's servants, agents of wrath to bring punishment on the wrongdoer" (13:4 NIV). Clearly he was thinking of legitimate governments that, while having some problematic features, have the goal of administering justice.

Obviously, it should be the goal of every government to govern justly, though they sometimes don't. Also obviously, it should be the goal of every human judge to reflect the perfect judgment of a perfect God according to his perfect laws. Here's where the challenging claim and question of Abraham stands out. For if the Judge of all the *earth* does right, then surely the judges of this or that smaller jurisdiction should do right in imitation of the divine Judge. The LORD himself should be the earthly judge's model.

This model exists whether any particular judge is a person accepting the tenets of Judaism, Christianity, or any religious faith. The self-revelation of God in history has resulted in the existence of moral standards that come from him. As a result, standards of justice may be applied by courts according to the laws of their nations and states, and those standards are remarkably similar from place to place, especially in the major issues of law—possession of property, violence to persons, etc.

Nevertheless, I don't ignore the differences in laws around the globe; my purpose is to follow the revelation of godly principles of justice that descend from the revelation of God through the Bible. The principles of the judiciary, as God expects judges to follow them, are written throughout the Old and New Testaments, the history of the Israelites and the message of Christianity respectively.

One of the stated goals of judges throughout our republic is a nearly word-for-word recitation of a biblical command.

Do Justice and Justice Alone

In South Carolina, the State's adopted Court Rules contain the Judge's Oath, a 137 word oath the summary statement of which is: "I pledge to seek justice, and justice alone." I remember the day I took that oath, and I remember feeling the solemnity and importance of that oath at least as much as in my taking my marriage vows. This was not just a job I was undertaking: it was a holy duty.

The phrase occurs in the Bible, in Deuteronomy:

Follow justice and justice alone, so that you may live and possess the land the LORD your God is giving you (Deuteronomy 16:20 NIV).

A word-for-word translation of the Hebrew in this verse actually says, "Justice justice you shall follow." The Hebrew construction is an intensifier. In English we use other words to mean the same thing. The NIV renders it as we might well say it, while other translations often have, "Justice and only justice," or "What is altogether just."

Justice is paramount

The emphatic point for the judge in the Bible's command is that the goal of justice should be in front of him at every step, never fading from his sight. In every ruling, every finding, every decision or verdict, and in sentencing or awarding, justice must be his devoted goal. Justice is paramount.

This paramount consideration, which summarizes all the other pledges the judge makes in his oath, is what makes sidetracks and competing goals so insidious. There are political issues that sometimes creep into cases through the claims of a Complaint or the people involved. There are community personalities waiting to take offense and self-appointed leaders of social issues implicitly threatening negative public opinion of the court. Sometimes, unfortunately, there are other judges who will express disagreement. The judge must not be deterred in pursuing justice and justice alone.

Often the distraction from justice that threatens it the most is fear, at some level sufficient to tempt the judge to rule differently from what he would otherwise.

I once took a civil case, a suit for $800, on transfer from a nearby judge who recused himself on the claim that he was prejudiced. Actually, this was the claim of the defendant, who filed a motion petitioning the judge to recuse. The judge, a friend of mine, was frankly glad to do so since he had had his fill of the defendant in previous hearings on the matter. Conveniently, he regarded his feelings as prejudicial, and asked if I would take the case. I or some other judge should have been assigned the case by the chief magistrate of the county, but things in the magisterial courts often operated on an informal level, and I agreed to accept the case.

The day he personally brought over the inch-and-a-half thick file on the case, as he handed it to me he said, "Watch your back." I soon learned what my judge friend had been dealing with. The defendant was a so-called "sovereign citizen," who was using every legal maneuver he could come up with—often with no real legitimacy—to tie up the court in procedural matters and frustrate the purpose of justice. The core issue was payment of some homeowner association fees. I had handled many HOA cases, filed by either homeowner or association. What made this one different was that the homeowner had adopted a political position in which he claimed his land was not subject to the laws of the state. In fact, he had elected himself governor of his own property.

Sovereign citizens are not generally known for initiating violent acts, but rather for falsifying various documents, including driver's licenses and automobile license plates. The FBI says some sovereign citizens produce counterfeit currency. But when law enforcement gets involved, sovereign citizens have been known to become violent.

I had attended seminars about the sovereign citizen movement. And I knew there was a pocket of them in the northern part of my county, where this particular defendant lived. Added to that, the northern part of the county had been known for two hundred years as "the Dark Corner," conjuring up justified images of backwoods miscreants "taking care of" people who threaten their way of life.

"Watch your back."

I thought I had been relieved of the entire case when the defendant filed a further countersuit alleging millions of dollars in damages. The amount exceeded my court's jurisdiction, and I sent the case to the circuit court. But in another few months, it came back to me, the countersuit dismissed and the monetary claims now back to $800.00. I scheduled a trial on the issues.

Before the date arrived, a friend of mine who was an officer in the Department of Natural Resources, and whose "beat" was regularly the northern area of the county, stopped by with a ticket to file. In conversation he became serious and said something to the effect that 'you never know what those boys (sovereign citizens) are gonna do.'

Well, thanks for more reason to fear that ruling against the defendant was potentially dangerous.

When the trial took place, the evidence was clearly, and entirely, on the side of the plaintiff, the HOA. "Watch your back." I ruled for the plaintiff and ordered the defendant to pay the HOA $800.00. Then I waited, wondering if in a few days or weeks there might be reprisals. I didn't know what to expect.

The defendant didn't pay the HOA. The defendant further defaulted on his mortgage. His bank foreclosed on his house and property. The day came when the sheriff had to take a team of men out to the property, which the homeowner had barricaded off. The matter never resulted in gunfire. The homeowner moved somewhere unknown to me. A few months passed. I had received no threats. I assumed I was in the clear.

Then a large envelope came in the mail to the courthouse. It was a lawsuit, naming the judge who had originally handled the case, all his staff, various other people connected to the case through his court, and also *my* staff, and *me*. The amount of the suit was multiple millions of dollars.

Apparently I had no reason to fear physical violence from this man, who had a nice looking family (they had all come to court), and who himself looked more like a CPA or a minister than some violence-prone hillbilly. His weapon of choice was a lawsuit. Had I had reason to anticipate a lawsuit, the temptation to let his bizarre claims affect my disposition of the case might have raised fears of a different kind.

"Watch your back."

The lawsuit was instead a full frontal assault. Fortunately for me it was fraught with problems, starting with the fact that the plaintiff had attempted to serve the suit himself, which is invalid. He also failed to understand that judges, and by extension their staffs, have immunity from lawsuits for things they do in the course of their office. There were other flaws, and the county attorney who defended the other judge, me, and our staffs, was able to get the entire matter dismissed within a short period of time.

But the threat, however brief, had brought up a host of fears in my mind, memories of a lawsuit filed against me and my wife years before, over a car accident my wife was in. It was my first—and I had hoped, my only— experience with being sued, and it had kept me up nights worrying about how I would be able to pay a judgment for anything near what the plaintiff in that case was asking. Fortunately also in that case, the matter was dismissed before going to trial.

I hadn't been threatened with a lawsuit by this sovereign citizen. Instead, I had heard an undercurrent of intimidating things about him or his friends implying violence, and my fellow judge had solemnly warned me, "Watch your back."

Through it all, I had reminded myself, Do justice and justice alone. I didn't have to tiptoe around matters or deny plaintiff's rights, though I remember being impassive and without any trace of insult or ridicule of the defendant's bizarre political views. I just had to commit myself to my God and do justice. Justice was paramount.

The paramount nature of justice is not simply a reminder to normally just judges of good character. In the Bible, the matter of the supreme importance of justice is often expressed in prophetic utterances about the fact that the prophets' hearers were anything but just to begin with. As a result, the poor, often the ultimate casualties in society, were being victimized by the very system meant to protect citizens.

Justice for powerless victims

One of the recurring themes of the Old Testament prophets was the injustice of national leaders and indeed the entire spectrum of administrators of the justice system. Amos was no exception to these prophets:

You persecute good people, take bribes, and prevent the poor from getting justice in the courts (Amos 5:12 GNT).

In all likelihood the charge of persecuting good people was aimed at officials who leveled charges or applied laws in a repressive way. The prophets sometimes don't give us enough details to identify specific illustrations of what was going on, but we may be sure their hearers knew what they were talking about.

The effect of these accusations in a general form is that the reader in any age can't read about a specific case in the Bible and say to himself that nothing about it applies to him. The general accusations of persecution invite inspection of a country or culture to see where the "powers that be" victimize people, especially the poor and powerless.

The accusation of taking bribes is, of course, quite specific, and bribery is sometimes a more blunt but accurate word to describe all the "benefits" to be had by legislators from the generous hands of "special interests" or lobbyists. There is no way to estimate how immensely significant the effect this kind of activity has had on the making of laws.

Nor have courts been immune. For many years, one of the recurring themes of the television and movie making industry has been that judges often take bribes. My belief is that the general impression left by TV and movies is misleading as to the extent of the bribery of judges, but I don't know of a source of statistics to support my belief. Any records of cases where judges have been charged with taking bribes would lack information about incidents no one has yet found out about. Still, I think the entertainment industry exaggerates, not unlike they do when they typify southern Protestant ministers as charlatans or Catholic priests as child molesters.

Where the ancient, Jewish courts shared blame was in failing to see that justice was finally done in cases coming before them where people, often very poor, had been victimized by the rich and/or powerful. We can be sure that this kind of inequity occurred when judges sided with the powerful in their claims or defenses.

It's legitimate to ask ourselves whether judges who "prevented the poor from getting justice in the courts" did so while fully knowing they were not being fair, or whether, so fully immersed in a system of reciprocity between leaders and administrators, they had simply come to see things the way their friends did. With such a biased conditioning of their minds—and indeed, their hearts— their concept of justice might have become so weighted toward the rich and powerful, of whom they were part, that the claims or defenses of the have-nots in their courts simply could not prevail.

In the end, it doesn't matter. Whether one is unjust because he falls prey in the moment to an unusual temptation to go against what he knows somewhere inside him is right, or because he has become so thoroughly immersed in his biases, prejudices and loyalties that he doesn't recognize injustice when he does it, in either case he is culpable. He has become part of the enemy of the good.

The prophet had more to say about injustice:

You people hate anyone who challenges injustice and speaks the whole truth in court (Amos 5:10 GNT).

The context of this verse is the same as the passage two verses later, involving the poor, and the injustice spoken of probably had to do with how the have-nots were frequently victimized by the haves, with the full complicity of the courts. The opposite circumstance, of course, could be in view. Those challenging injustice might have been litigants bringing claims before judges on behalf of the have-nots against the haves. In such circumstances, Amos's critique would have meant that those entrenched in power saw to it that judges did not upset the status quo. It would be difficult to find examples of such legal activists in Israel, or probably in the ancient world in general.

Currently, however, we could think of examples of fearless prosecutors, as well as defenders, who champion causes of justice for the people at large, sometimes against special interests that have entwined themselves in the machinery of government resulting in public evils. Such champions are frequently vilified as much as they are applauded. And yes, sometimes these "champions" are simply lawyers who file class action suits, where vast numbers of "victims" are their cover for enriching themselves through the legal system.

I didn't see any notable challenges by legal champions against raging societal inequities in my court. But among the mundane matters that typified what came before me, there were occasional defendants, in particular, who presented cogent and credible defenses against plaintiffs who were abusive of their rights. A number of these were landlord-tenant cases, where landlords shortcut the requirements of landlord-tenant law and then brought suit for eviction when tenants didn't simply gather up their belongings and go.

I had a particular landlord who typically showed no regard for proper notice of breaches of lease, never giving his tenants the required time to cure those breaches. When he filed for eviction, we usually heard from his tenants with loud defenses. I dismissed more than a few cases where he had violated the law. I warned this landlord—actually, I warned his daughter, who handled almost all the business for her aging father—but the warnings didn't seem to take. Eventually, the man died, his daughter hired a professional property manager—which her penny-pinching father would never do—and I never had another eviction case filed by them again.

What is notable about the message of most of the Old Testament prophets in the matter of justice is how focused they were on the core issues. As we say sometimes today, they kept the main thing the main thing. There were certainly procedural matters in the courts of their day, though in all likelihood nowhere near what we have in our times. That fact makes it all the more important that the justice system in its entirety, and the judge in particular, focus on the end result of justice.

Justice over procedure

One of the memorable confrontations Jesus had with opponents in the New Testament was with a collection of religious leaders who found fault with him at almost every turn. Matthew's gospel records the encounter:

> **Woe unto you, scribes and Pharisees, hypocrites! for ye pay tithe of mint and anise and cummin, and have omitted the weightier matters of the law, judgment, mercy, and faith: these ought ye to have done, and not to leave the other undone (Matthew 23:23 KJV).**

Readers must understand the place of religious law, sometimes called tradition, in the life of Israel. In the time of Jesus, Israel— the territory of Judea—was under Roman rule and law, but it had its own laws as well, which Rome expected it to handle in its own courts. Much of this law came out of their scriptures (what Christians call the Old Testament), but to these moral laws the scribes, Pharisees and others had added rules for just about every conceivable event or action. Their commentaries on the scriptures had acquired the weight of law, at least in their assessment.

The number of things Jews had to do to conform to these expectations was burdensome. Jesus and his disciples were castigated, for instance, because they skipped various hand washings that the Pharisees required on the notion that they made people "clean." Ceremonial cleanliness was a major consideration in Jewish life. But while the Pharisees and scribes were super attentive to performing all these rituals, they had "omitted" (Jesus didn't even say "de-emphasized") what was far more important, which was what the prophets had always preached as God's chief expectation: justice (KJV "judgment"), mercy and faith.

The parallel is not exact, but the comparison is illustrative. It is possible for legal cases to become bogged down in procedure to the point that justice is, at the very least, de-emphasized.

The theory of magistrate court in South Carolina includes the notion that procedure is pared down, that it is simpler for citizens to seek legal redress than in higher courts. They don't have to have attorneys, though they may choose to. If they need help filling out forms, a magistrate is instructed under magistrate court rules to offer that help, which usually means a court clerk does it. Litigants don't have to know a lot about how to present their case at trial, though some take on the challenge and do a remarkable job of it.

But I had a plaintiff once who said first thing in court that he didn't know what he was doing and he asked me to ask him questions. Actually, under the court rules I was required to ask questions of unrepresented parties to make sure all claims or defenses were presented. So I looked at his Complaint form and asked him a series of questions covering all his issues with the defendant. (When it came to the defendant, I made sure he felt equally satisfied that he had said all he came to say!) What was important was not that they sounded like lawyers and used all the terms and made motions—procedure—but that justice was done. And it was.

Usually, however, the tendency for procedure to overshadow justice takes place in higher courts. In fact one of the more famous issues of what rightly is classified as procedure is an issue that may get a second and revolutionary look by the Supreme Court. Justice Thomas suggested that the Court should look at the federal exclusionary rule, which bars the admission of evidence collected as a result of a warrant-less search.

The rule goes back to 1914. Its purpose was to uphold the protections of the Fourth Amendment to the Constitution. But what it required often meant the elimination of the government's case. It led to the well known phrase, "the fruit of the poisonous tree." Justice Thomas says the Supreme Court has no power to force states to adopt the rule themselves. In practice, however, the exclusionary rule is very much the accepted operating procedure of courts all the way down to the Summary Court. I heard the occasional motion for exclusion of evidence on this basis, myself.

Where this procedural matter has its greatest impact on the actual performance of justice is not in its hand-slapping of police, but in its resulting dismissal of charges against some of the most deplorable criminals in our society. The procedural cure for overly eager police hardly seems just when compared to the dastardly evils their targets committed.

But the exclusionary rule, while it may finally be decided to have aided the escape of criminals for the sake of a technicality, at least did have justice as its intention. The wonderful summations of American citizens' rights under the Fourth and other Amendments have been interpreted many times over the years, expanding our understanding of how justice should be done in our country. In a word, it should be done by intention, as a quest.

Justice as a quest

The prophet Isaiah spoke the word of God to Israel through

the course of several royal administrations, and his message was much like that of most of the other prophets in the period of Israel's history prior to their defeat and captivity in Babylon. That captivity was in their future because since the time of the reigns of David and Solomon, Israel had become increasingly idolatrous, unjust, and oppressive. Judgment was coming from the Judge on high, and the prophets gave the reasons repeatedly. They also passionately challenged the nation as to how they should live by contrast:

> **…Learn to do good; seek justice, correct oppression; bring justice to the fatherless, plead the widow's cause (Isaiah 1:17 ESV).**

This message echoed King Lemuel's writing years before:

> **Open your mouth for the mute, for the rights of all who are destitute. Open your mouth, judge righteously, defend the rights of the poor and needy (Proverbs 31:8-9 ESV).**

The justice system of the Israelites was not like that of America or any nation not functioning as a theocracy. The prophets sometimes proclaimed the need of an advocacy system where the court itself could initiate judgments, unlike our system in a democratic republic where either the executive branch (police and district attorneys, etc.) must initiate a case to the judiciary or a citizen must bring a case against another citizen.

But if we ignore for a moment the origin of the case, the responsibility still lies in the court to take the opportunity of any case to seek justice and not bend to the will of the powerful or the rich simply because they are so. Our system should not shortchange society's needful persons. In a word, judges should daily be on a quest to do justice.

This is the reason that our courts must question defendants in criminal cases as to whether they want to be represented but cannot afford a lawyer. One of the main reasons I had to continue a case in my court was so that defendants could acquire a lawyer. In our county, that was done through the Office of Indigent Defense. Every once in a while someone would be given adequate information as to how to get free criminal defense and given adequate time to do so before coming back to a rescheduled hearing, but he/she would show up alone. I heard various excuses, but invariably in my experience these were people who thought they could delay the inevitable, and it didn't work in my courtroom. The truly needy would have representation; people trying to game the system wouldn't.

In other words, justice is a two way street. To serve its purposes, sometimes defendants must be found not guilty or not liable. Sometimes, the state must prevail, or justice will not be done.

Obviously, justice is not and should not be weighted on the side of either party in court, whether the trial is civil or criminal in nature. It might be concluded by a casual observer of some courtroom proceedings that a judge just rubber stamps the case of the state (or the city, in municipal trials) against all defendants. If that's actually taking place, then obviously justice isn't being done to somebody. In practice, however, it's probably true that in most jurisdictions, especially in courts handling misdemeanors as well as traffic cases, police or city or county attorneys don't show up with questionable cases they might lose. Their record of wins is a reflection of their having slam-dunk cases against defendants who unquestionably "dunnit."

This was the typical situation in my court, which handled all fraudulent checks for the county. The county solicitor had a program approved and ordered by the South Carolina Supreme Court under which a business, for instance, that had received a bad check could submit a claim for recovery. By itself, this program was part of a quest for justice: justice for victims of bad checks and justice for writers of the same. The solicitor's office sent out one letter, then another, escalating demand for payment. If the person made the check good through the program (and paid a fee), the case was closed. If not, the solicitor showed up at my court and sought arrest warrants.

The program allowed people to make payments through the solicitor's office even after arrest, up until a short time before scheduled trial. If they did, the case was *nolle prossed* (not prosecuted). What a deal! But even then, some people didn't pay, and they came to court.

The evidence the solicitor's office had to have even to *seek* a warrant in these cases was not merely "probable cause," but a full blown, prima facie case, which in the case of fraudulent checks is laid out in S.C. law itself. In other words, slam-dunk. But there were a few places where there might be unexpected holes in the case.

I might have a dozen or more bad check cases every month after the solicitor was able to collect on five or ten times that many during the past several weeks. And normally, those cases would go quickly because of the threshold of even bringing those defendants into court. The check writer would be found guilty, fined and ordered to make restitution.

But then sometimes one of those "holes" would show up. Usually it took the form of a defendant's testimony that he didn't write the check. In several cases I didn't have to wait for the defendant to try to prove the claim. I simply looked at what the state had given me and compared it to the forms I already had in the case file, such as a bond form containing the defendant's signature. Sometimes the inconsistency between signatures was glaring. Several times over the years I asked the solicitor to approach the bench and compare signatures, without prompting her. Then, usually without my even asking if there were any motion from the state, she would move to dismiss. These were times when both the state and the court were on a quest for justice.

This quest is also commanded by Jeremiah:

Administer justice every morning, and rescue the victim of robbery from the hand of his oppressor, or my anger will flare up like fire and burn unquenchably because of their evil deeds (Jeremiah 21:12 HCSB).

It was an oft repeated command in the Old Testament for the justice system to rectify inequities among victims of social ills, indicating the prevalence of these conditions in Israel leading up to the conclusive invasion by Babylon in 587 B.C. God considered the quest for justice to be vital to his people's very continuation as a nation.

Justice in Israel, when held to be paramount, and when pursued as a quest, had positive effects, as it would anywhere.

Justice as restorative

A society where justice is routinely not done, where crime prevails, where at some levels government fails or refuses to prosecute lawbreakers because the sheer number of them overwhelms the system—that's a society where chaos reigns. Amazingly, some leaders effectively encourage this chaos by their policies. Sometimes the officials who should be seeking justice for the people at large—the people hurt by lawbreaking—give up on the cause of justice citing lack of money or manpower.

But the principle of justice as the paramount societal concern does not change for lack of money. The benefits of justice are too important to forfeit:

When justice is done, it brings joy to the righteous but terror to evildoers (Proverbs 2:15 NIV).

This is the whole point of the justice system: to combat the chaos resulting from "anything goes" with the accomplishment of justice. If justice is *not* done, neither result—joy to the righteous or terror to evildoers—takes place.

The experience of Israel showed that, at least in their case, a point could be reached at which it was too late to restore justice and thus restore the nation to God's good graces. Israel seemed to be pushing its limits. Yet, to the last hour, the prophets suggested there might be a prayer of national salvation:

> **Hate what is evil, love what is right, and see that justice prevails in the courts. Perhaps the Lord will be merciful to the people of this nation who are still left alive (Amos 5:15 GNT).**

The ministry of Amos, quoted earlier, was focused much more on the injustice of his society than on its other various immoralities, though those were numerous and serious. In this passage, Amos basically concedes there will be a judgment on the nation, but he says there might be hope for the survivors of it.

Justice may be salvific
The hope of national salvation becomes quite relevant in times of moral ferment. The time of this author's writing is such a time. The list of perversions and national sins of Israel sounds eerily familiar when read two decades into the 21st century:

> **'So I will come to put you on trial. I will be quick to testify against sorcerers, adulterers and perjurers, against those who defraud laborers of their wages, who oppress the widows and the fatherless, and deprive the foreigners among you of justice, but do not fear me,' says the Lord Almighty (Malachi 3:5 NIV).**

For "sorcerers" read "witches" as the Brenton Septuigent Translation has it, or "all who practice witchcraft," as the CEV renders the word. The GNT has simply, "those who practice magic." The practice of sorcery (or divination) hasn't gone away;

it has simply changed names and traditions. The reader might be astounded at the number of people in the U.S. who identify themselves as witches. Some estimates put it at more than 1.5 million. Add the unknown number of Satanists and even the practitioners of tarot, the self-proclaimed psychics and the purveyors of holism, pantheism and occultism popularized in the now well-worn New Age movement. Satanists are trying to get their clubs allowed in schools, and current news indicates they are succeeding, even in elementary schools.

When you read of "perjurers" in Malachi, think of the number of national figures such as agency heads, who have lied to us, sometimes under oath to Congress, sometimes to hundreds of millions via television in bald faced denials of what we discover was true. Or think of the politicians who make glowing promises of things they never do.

"Adulterers" needs no updated interpretation. Adultery is rampant; fornication is the open rule rather than the secretive exception, especially among teens and young adults. And miscellaneous sexual perversions have exploded on the scene in the past two generations. Do not think that God is unconcerned about all this immorality.

The economic sins of the Israelites also have obvious parallels in modern times. Exploitation of people desperate for a meager living is something that takes place continually, for all the promises of politicians to wipe out poverty or to bridle the profiteers.

The prophet articulated the mind of God: "I will come put you on trial." Most translations have something like, "I will come near you in judgment." There is no question about the outcome of the trial. God has a prima facie case. Judgment is simply waiting in the wings.

Without fixed principles of truth and righteousness, immorality, injustice, and idolatry proliferate. In fact there *are* fixed principles; they simply are not recognized by the postmodernist culture of hedonism and expanding perversion that has emerged in the west, in the United States in particular.

The place of the courtroom in the battle against the increasingly godless culture is mostly in handling cases of rampant crime. The courts do not write the laws. Legislators do, and they are sometimes swayed by various social movements that sweep the populace into their murmuration of claimed moral superiority, which is sometimes immorality instead. The current idiocy of governmental support for gender transitioning, particularly for minors, is an example of good sense being overwhelmed by fear of "cancellation," as it has been called, or public shaming by a shouting minority that doesn't hesitate to create invective by adding "-phobic" to their latest immoral cause and labeling public figures with it.

Indeed, a few higher courts have participated in the interpretation of our national founding documents to imply things relating to the sexual liberation movement at which the founders would have been aghast. In such cases, lower courts are stuck with precedents they have little to no choice but to follow.

The Summary Court generally wages the ongoing cultural war by adjudicating cases of injustice at the personal level, misdemeanors and civil injustices. Otherwise, the magistrate judge just peers out at the roiling storm of cultural immorality, perversity and folly and wishes he could rap his gavel, bring it all to a halt, and order the country to behave.

The Judge Serves the People

At every level, one of the chief principles of the judiciary is that judges serve the people. They do not exist to serve themselves.

This principle may seem obvious, but the extent to which some judges conduct themselves and their courts suggests they may have gotten out of balance, using their courts to enhance their reputation and status, or treating parties as instruments of self-aggrandizement. It is vital for the judge to know his purpose and to fulfil it humbly.

Jesus was once asked to perform the duty of a judge:

And one of the company said unto him, Master, speak to my brother, that he divide the inheritance with me. And he said unto him, Man, who made me a judge or a divider over you? And he said unto them, Take heed, and beware of covetousness: for a man's life consisteth not in the abundance of the things which he possesseth (Luke 12:13-14 KJV).

Jesus did not come to be a local magistrate. His mission was otherwise; it had been given him by God the Father. The first answer he gave to the man was essentially that he would not take upon himself the role of legal arbiter. Considering the divine identity the New Testament claims about Jesus, it could be thought surprising that he would not weigh in on the matter brought to him, since his judgment would certainly have had the imprimatur of heaven itself. Yet he didn't. God the Father was in charge of Jesus' role.

Similarly, judges do not appoint themselves. They are appointed, elected, or nominated and confirmed, but they don't pick themselves for the judiciary. In my state, magisterial judges are nominated for the Summary Courts, then appointed by the governor. The selection of judges is a reflection of how the state, at the point that it designed the process, wished to express the fact that judges serve the people.

Not his own interests
An Old Testament story about a son of King David illustrates the pursuit of influence and power:

Absalom …would get up early and stand by the side of the road leading to the city gate. Whenever anyone came with a complaint to be placed before the king for a decision, Absalom would call out to him, "What town are you from?" He would answer, "Your servant is from one of the tribes of Israel." Then Absalom

would say to him, "Look, your claims are valid and proper, but there is no representative of the king to hear you." And Absalom would add, "If only I were appointed judge in the land! Then everyone who has a complaint or case could come to me and I would see that they receive justice." ...and so he stole the hearts of the people of Israel (2 Samuel 15:2-6 NIV).

Absalom coveted the position of judge, in fact, the highest bench in the land. Actually, he wanted to use even that position as a final stairstep to the throne. It was Absalom's intention to use the position of judge—whether he acquired it officially or unofficially—to convince people that he was a better source of justice than his father the king. The strategy worked, and it led to civil war.

It's common for judges to talk about "*my* courtroom" or "*my* court." In fact, court administrations often encourage judges to develop the kind of order in their courtrooms that engenders respect for the law and for the authority of the judge. To the extent that judges are acting with this purpose, their courts *are* theirs.

However, if a judge runs roughshod over the rights of parties, or shortchanges defendants, for example, of full hearing by applying court rules—to say nothing of their own—in a draconian manner, his protection of the sanctity of his court has become a sense of ownership. In a state of over three hundred magistrate courts, I knew of a few where the judge acted more like a medieval lord over his fiefdom than a judge serving his state.

Not to enrich himself

During regular training sessions, among the many things the Court Administration regularly urged magistrates of my state to remember was the vital importance of honest fiscal management. There was always a note of warning by the various instructors who conducted ethics training, and the training itself was required annually. Presentations by the legal staff of the State Supreme Court's Court Administration included reading off the names of judges who had been disciplined or removed for one of several causes. Among the chief ways a magistrate could offend was in financial mismanagement. Sometimes, "mismanagement" was just another word for "theft." It could have been misappropriation of fees—stealing from the county. It could have been taking payments from the public, such as honorariums for services not required —stealing from the public.

A judge who diverts funds for himself has violated the sacred trust given him by the people, to serve them, not himself.

By law, a magistrate is held responsible for financial mismanagement even if a member of his staff committed theft without his knowledge or collusion. The staff member probably would be prosecuted, while the judge might only be subject to some level of discipline, to include removal from office. But that's why it was my regular practice to look at the books every month, to make certain the numbers added up right, and to meet with county officials when the books were audited. The last thing I wanted was to be hoodwinked into believing that all was well, only to have auditors discover that somebody in my office was embezzling. Fortunately for me, my regular looks at the books verified that my people were trustworthy, a fact of which I never had any doubt.

Most years I served as a judge, state authorities praised our statewide system for the low, and lowering, numbers of judicial sanctions. It wasn't always true in our past. And it wasn't true in every state—we looked at the statistics from around the country. The situation has sometimes been reminiscent of what one Old Testament prophet must have been thinking when he wrote:

...her judges are wolves of the night, which leave nothing for the morning (Zephaniah 3:3 CSB).

While a problem of a magnitude that could be described with such extreme terms would be more likely to occur today in a proverbial "banana republic" than the 21st century United States, it isn't impossible for it to take place. But the very purpose of oversight commissions and committees for the judiciary in this country is to keep the ever present temptation of graft and theft from taking hold among our judges.

Service through upholding law, not making it

Not only is the courtroom not his to do with as the judge pleases, but the law that is the business of the court is not his to make; legislators make it. This seems painfully obvious, but it's simply another way of saying that the judge must not play fast and loose with the law, and that he must know it in order to apply it.

An interesting conversation took place between Jesus and Jewish leaders as recorded in the gospel of John. The leaders persistently contested Jesus' right to say and do the things he did.

I can of mine own self do nothing: as I hear, I judge: and my judgment is just; because I seek not mine own will, but the will of the Father which hath sent me (John 5:30 KJV).

This passage doesn't appear at first glance really to be about the judiciary. We've already noted that Jesus disavowed any appointment by God to be an earthly judge (Luke 12:13-14). However, we should look at this passage as being about the activity Jesus was engaged in rather than a position he held—or rather, did not hold. He was not a "magistrate" (see Luke 12:58), but in the passage where he made these remarks to Jewish leaders he had listened to them make their case for his not healing on the Sabbath.

In response, Jesus performed the adversarial role as if in court, saying, "My Father worketh hitherto, and I work." When the Jewish leaders countered with the argument that he was making himself equal with God (the Father), Jesus replied, "The Son can do nothing of himself, but what he seeth the Father do: for what things soever he doeth, these also doeth the Son likewise."

Each side having rested, Jesus now said, "The Father …hath committed all judgment unto the Son," and he gave his judgment about them: they didn't honor the Son; they didn't honor the Father; and they didn't have God's word abiding in them.

Jesus had made judgments about any number of Jewish regulations that did not have the force of Old Testament law: he had declared all foods clean; he had declared hand-washing "laws" invalid; he had declared the Sabbath as made for man instead of man for the Sabbath, specifically allowing people to be healed on the Sabbath day.

But note that in all cases where he rendered judgment, he did *not* make the law, the divine standard, according to which he rendered judgment. He said, "I can of mine own self do nothing: as I hear, I judge: and my judgment is just; because I seek not mine own will, but the will of the Father which hath sent me." What he "heard" was the Father's word—the divine instruction, the divine law. And in seeking "not mine own will," he was abiding by that divine law.

The long Johannine passages in which Jesus sorts out the truth from the invalid reasoning of the scribes and Pharisees sometimes seem circuitous and confusing—most people think today's legal arguments or judicial decisions are equally complex and difficult to understand. But the principle was clear: Jesus, God the Son Incarnate, while possessing all the prerogatives of God, did not exercise them while on earth, instead deferring to God the Father for the authority to act as judge to be given to him.

The application of this Bible passage to our subject is straightforward: the human judge has the limited function of *applying* the law (based on his findings from evidence). In his judgment on an issue he is upholding the law, not making it, and he is confined to what the law says.

This principle, however, cuts both ways. If the judge doesn't make laws that aren't there, in order to support his decisions, he is equally responsible to know what laws *do exist*, so he can apply them.

Early in my years as a magistrate I attended a training session where numerous topics were covered in the three days we were there. One presentation was on the subject of Claim and Delivery law. For readers who are not lawyers or judges, a Claim and Delivery action is a very old legal remedy coming out of English common law in which a person lays *claim* to some property for which he says he has the right of possession, and petitions the court to *deliver* the property to him. The training session was designed to walk the judges through the steps laid out in the law to handle such an action. There were forms for use at every step.

What was presented as the last step was the court's Order of Dispossession, which a constable would take to the location of the property where he would seize the property, to deliver it to the Plaintiff. A new judge (newer than I!) asked what would happen if the property wasn't there. The presenter was someone I had seen often at these training events, and this wasn't her specific field of expertise. She deferred to the class for an answer, and one old judge (considerably more experienced than I!) piped up:

"The plaintiff would have to file another action with the court, to sue for the value of the property."

The presenter seemed satisfied with the judge's answer —actually, she seemed grateful that he had answered since she didn't know. No one else had anything to say in disagreement.

I, on the other hand—and I confess to tooting my own horn, here—*was* an expert in Claim and Delivery law, even in my relatively short career as a judge. I dealt with it every day, and I could quote most parts of the law from the South Carolina Code. So, *I* piped up myself. I said that actually the plaintiff didn't have to spend even more money and waste even more time getting paid for what his property had been worth (a typical item of property was a car). I quoted from the law:

The judgment for the plaintiff may be for the possession,

the recovery of the possession or *the value thereof* in case a delivery cannot be had and for damages for the detention" (S.C. Code of Laws, Section 22-3-1460, *emphasis mine*).

In his years on the bench there's no telling how many Claim and Delivery actions this venerable judge had handled, probably quite a few of them where the property had been sold, was broken and thrown away, or had been hidden so it couldn't be reclaimed. If he required plaintiffs in those cases to file again for a monetary judgment, then two things had happened:

a. The judge had made up law himself, whereby a plaintiff had to file a new action for money; and
b. The judge had essentially invalidated the existing law by failing to know it and apply it.

In either case, the rights of the citizen were violated.

The most significant, and potentially egregious, examples of judges making law are not, of course, at the lower court levels but at the level of state supreme courts and the U.S. Supreme Court. Now and then SCOTUS has dipped into the waters of law making rather than interpreting and upholding. Sometimes its novel rulings have been applauded almost universally and still are. Sometimes its virtually law-making decisions have brought continuing division and a lingering sense of trouble.

However, there is a divine directive to judges to be conscious of injustice and alert to possibilities *within their rightful role* to right wrongs. The Bible speaks repeatedly to this mindfulness of judges:

Speak up for those who cannot speak for themselves, for the rights of all who are destitute. Speak up and judge fairly; defend the rights of the poor and needy (Proverbs 31:8-9 NIV).

I do not advocate judicial activism. I do not believe judges should find in the law what was not intended by legislators. That said, there is a time for a judge to see basic issues of human rights or citizen rights in cases that come before him. If the larger picture of justice is suffering violence, rectifying the smaller picture without regard to how it may contribute to the larger one is failure to speak up for the true victims.

The larger picture of justice is often where the most egregious wrongs take place. One only has to think of the Dred Scott decision by the U.S. Supreme Court in 1857, which extended the national crime against Blacks in America. Or Plessy v. Ferguson in 1896, which led to Jim Crow laws, severely segregating Blacks. Scores of other SCOTUS cases are thought to be unjust by some segment of society—the 2022 decision in Dobbs v. Jackson, which overturned the decision in Roe v. Wade, for instance—but the ones I've just cited are nearly universally agreed to have been very, very bad decisions by very badly misguided judges about the national sin of slavery and the position of Blacks as citizens in this country.

While the lowly magistrate doesn't have any influence over the Justices of the Supreme Court, there would be many stories that could be told where lower court judges handled cases that were appealed, appealed higher, and finally reached SCOTUS, where perhaps the judgment of the original court was upheld. In such cases, the vital importance of the lower—dare I say the lowest?—court's rendering a supremely just verdict would be immensely important. It could be the decision that ignited a fuse the set off a firestorm that set right some great injustice. The judge never knows.

What often alerts people, judges along with them, to a growing problem of injustice is widespread public notice and public discontent. Isaiah addressed such situations:

Woe to those who enact evil statutes and to those who constantly record unjust decisions, so as to deprive the needy of justice and rob the poor of my people of their rights, so

that widows may be their spoil and that they may plunder the orphans (Isaiah 10:1-2 NASB 1977).

The reader is inclined to shake his head and wonder who would possibly be guilty of making admittedly evil laws, just so a class of the powerful could deprive other people of their rights, and so they could get rich off of widows and orphans. In fact, how does one get rich off the poor, anyway?

If we read the verses that way, we miss the point. Isaiah was not saying that the people who made the law thought of themselves as wicked, or that their evaluation of the statutes they made was that they were evil. He was saying that like it or not, that's what they were. And he wasn't saying the powerful set out to rob people of their rights, only that that's what they were really doing. And they didn't think of themselves as taking even more of this world's goods from the hands and homes of widows and orphans, but that was, in fact, what they were doing.

In Isaiah's day there weren't political parties. In our day, of course, there are, and the two major parties—really, all of them—engage in a constant battle to typify, even to the point of caricaturing, the beliefs and actions of the competing parties as blatantly evil. Democrats are famous for saying that Republicans are trying to starve children and rob the elderly of government benefits. Republicans accuse Democrats of uniformly being in the pocket of special interests and wanting to bankrupt the country through higher taxes. The germ of truth is lost in the unjustified exaggeration.

Or think of the recent SCOTUS decision overturning Roe v. Wade. In the larger abortion debate, supporters of abortion claim its opponents are fascists wanting to deny women their rights. Opponents of abortion claim its supporters (most specifically those who obtain abortions) are murderers of unborn babies. But when they hunt for some term for themselves, opponents of abortion call themselves "pro life," while supporters of abortion call themselves "pro choice." We have a habit, don't we, of labeling ourselves positively and our opponents negatively?!

This is not to say in any national debate—and national debates tend to be intensely local—that there isn't a right and a wrong to be perceived. I'm not in the least suggesting that there isn't a right side and a wrong side in the abortion debate, the homosexual marriage issue, or any other national issue, going back to slavery and further in the past. And it's the quest for what is just and what is morally right that leads eventually to some resolution in most cases.

That quest makes it doubly important, as I said above, that the judge, no matter how low his court, be watchful for issues involving not just local ordinances or state laws or even federal laws, and not even just U.S. Constitutional issues, but divine laws as well. Some of those have been ensconced in the Constitution in the First Amendment, where our founders recognized our freedom of religion. As we move into the second half of the third century of our country's grand experiment, we will definitely be facing major challenges to the right of Christians to practice their faith in this country. Where a baker can be told he can't decline to promote someone's lifestyle through cake designs, when the baker's religion—no obscure faith, at that—declares that lifestyle to be immoral, then no end is in sight to the injustices that could be worked on Christians. A judge should be able to recognize when laws are really "evil statutes" designed to protect what is wrong or to prohibit what is manifestly right.

Three other scripture passages touch on the judge's not making law but applying it:

> **...for when your judgments are in the land, the inhabitants of the world will learn righteousness. But if the wicked man is shown favor, he does not learn righteousness. In a righteous land he acts unjustly and does not see the majesty of the Lord (Isaiah 26:9-10 HCSB).**

The passage appears to describe a nation where the worship and service of God is dominant. The influence of Christian faith in America, for instance, was significantly stronger at its founding and through the 19ᵗʰ century than it is today. The contrast drawn by v.10 ("But…") is that when wickedness is not only tolerated but celebrated, the populace is less and less guided by fixed truth. In other words, when the devoted opponents of Christian faith—or indeed all religious influence—have succeeded in getting the government to turn protection of religious freedom into equal discrimination against all religion, morals plummet and standards cease more and more to exist.

Or consider the prophet Hosea's take on the unjust character of kings:

> **They make many promises, take false oaths and make agreements; therefore lawsuits spring up like poisonous weeds in a plowed field (Hosea 10:4 NIV).**

We don't know the particulars of Hosea's general references, but the core idea is clear: when leaders are less and less the best moral examples in the country, chaos grows in the populace.

Finally, in the New Testament, another passage from John's gospel:

> **You judge according to the flesh; I am not judging anyone. But even if I do judge, my judgment is true, for I am not alone in it, but I and the Father who sent me (John 8:15-16 NASB).**

Recalling what we said on John 5:30, this passage further explains how Jesus appealed to the Father as the source of the law. And Jesus wasn't referring only to the law of Moses or the law of the Jews. He was referring to that ideal, universal law, fixed standards of right and wrong. Applying what Jesus said, the human judge is not to categorize persons unfairly or make snap judgments on the basis of appearance or first impressions, but instead to rely on evidence and go by the law as written.

Finally, as part of the principle of the judge's serving the people, there is an educational and disciplinary role:

Go to the Levitical priests and to the judge who is in office at that time. Inquire of them and they will give you the verdict. You must act according to the decisions they give you… Be careful to do everything they instruct you to do. …Anyone who shows contempt for the judge or for the priest who stands ministering there to the Lord your God is to be put to death. You must purge the evil from Israel. All the people will hear and be afraid, and will not be contemptuous again (Deuteronomy 17:8-13 NIV).

Some of what is in this passage is unique to Israel—for example, that priests were judges, or that contempt brought the death penalty. Generally, however, the instructions port over into secular governments and courts through the principles derived, two of which are:

- Litigants should learn in their culture that they must respect the courts and follow their decisions. This lesson should be inculcated in youth during school years. Sadly, it appears that "Civics" is a course not being universally taught to teens.
- Contempt of the court is ultimately contempt for the government of your nation. Since government is of God (Romans 12:1f), contempt for a just court is certainly rebellion against the Almighty.

The principles of the judiciary as we have looked at them address judges as a body and the theory of the judicial role. The Bible's attention to the subject of judges gets even more specific, as we shall see.

41

The Character of the Judge

My observation, and perhaps the reader's as well, is that judges in television and movie depictions are notoriously bad. I repeat this point, which I made in the previous chapter, because I believe contradicting this popular view is justified. Judges on the screen are frequently rude, condescending, and ill-tempered. While they demand no one else show contempt, they may themselves be contemptuous, of attorneys and others. And when the dramas depicting them reveal what's going on in their lives, judges are often immoral characters, carrying on sexual affairs, being blackmailed for the same, taking bribes or being corrupt in some other manner. If the viewer's opinion of judges in this country is influenced significantly by TV and movies, it's a very low opinion.

I believe a low estimation of the character and quality of judges *in general* in this nation is unjustified. I know of no central database that would prove or disprove my belief, but my contact with judges at my level, at the circuit court level, and indeed at the S.C. Supreme Court level, leads me to believe that what you see on television is a gross distortion.

One contributing factor to the generally high quality of judges in this country must be the oversight they are under in their various states, generally controlled by the supreme courts in those states. In our state the oversight body is the Court Administration of South Carolina. Not only do oversight bodies conduct ethics training for judges (required annually in SC), but also the existence of these administrative bodies and their sobering reports of judges warned, suspended or removed from office, serve as a deterrent to unethical behavior.

My purpose in this book is not to review the guidance or admonishment of the state with regard to judges, but to consult an even higher source of moral and ethical expectation. In spite of the fact that judges in my state and around the nation can be found to hold different religious views or accept no religion at all, I make no apology for appealing to the power and self-evident truth of the Bible. Its message is that the ultimate source of justice is God himself.

The Judge Must Be Just

We may say defensibly that above all other character qualifications for the judge is that he be just—not merely just in his dealings, but just, himself, as a person. Just dealings regularly proceed from just character. Furthermore, the obligation of a human judge to be just is based ultimately on the heavenly model.

Because God is just
In arguing his case against a popular excuse for not believing the gospel of Jesus Christ, Paul the Apostle appealed to the biblical view of God:

> **But if our unrighteousness brings out God's righteousness more clearly, what shall we say? That God is unjust in bringing his wrath on us? (I am using a human argument.) Certainly not! If that were so, how could God judge the world? (Romans 3:5-6 NIV).**

Some people in Rome hearing the gospel had apparently argued that if what some Christians said was true, that God is ultimately glorified by everything, then how come he punishes sin? Wouldn't that be unjust? Paul's counter argument was simply to assert that God is perfectly just with no exception. If he weren't, he wouldn't be in a position to judge the world.

Clearly God must be utterly just in order to judge us to the uttermost. Similarly, a human judge, though he cannot be perfect, must be an upright person. While it is not impossible for a judge who is not himself predominantly just to render just verdicts in court, (1) it is less likely that he will, and (2) the public's confidence in him will be eroded by their knowledge of his or her life of impropriety, immorality or crime. Judges are frequently removed for what to some people would seem like minor infractions, in order to uphold the high expectations of them.

Jesus' parable of the unjust judge (Luke 18:1-8) made its point about God's righteous treatment of petitioners by comparing him to an unjust earthly judge. Jesus' description of him was that he "feared not God, neither regarded man" (KJV). Other translations have "respected" for "regarded" and the NIV switches things around and says, "nor cared what people thought." All these translations are getting at the meaning of the Greek words *anthrōpon mé entrepomenos*. In practice it means someone who doesn't care much about other people. And as the NIV renders it, other people in turn don't think much of him, either.

This lack of concern or care for other people is what Jesus said typified what he then called the "unjust judge" (v.6). But there was another description of this judge; in fact it was the first description, that he "feared not God." All English translations have "fear" for the Greek word, which means not merely, or even especially, being afraid of God, but rather possessing a deep and sobering respect and awe for the person of a holy God who is aware of our deepest thoughts and is the supreme Judge of all the earth (see Genesis 18:25).

By taking the inverse of these descriptions we may arrive at a biblical view of the top recommendations for human judges. They may be expected to be just persons and, commensurately, just in their dealings with others.

Not just in court

A close relationship exists between the just character of the judge and the just quality of his judgments in court, or, indeed, the just quality of his judgments—assessments, opinions, determinations—of people anywhere, not just in court. Jesus drew this connection in his teaching about judging others:

> **...if a boy can be circumcised on the Sabbath so that the law of Moses may not be broken, why are you angry with me for healing a man's whole body on the Sabbath? Stop judging by mere appearances, but instead judge correctly (John 7:23-24 NIV).**

Various Jewish officials criticized Jesus for healing on the Sabbath, yet they would have thought nothing of performing circumcision on the Sabbath when it was the eighth day since the boy's birth. In other words, they made an exception for a ritual that Jesus said was far less important than healing human beings. In a word, they were being hypocrites. This hypocrisy was what lay at the root of their chronic and significantly unjust judgment—in this case, of Jesus himself.

Consequently, the biblical argument is that people engaging in judgment of others—whether casually or in the formal setting of a court—must avoid hypocrisy as part of developing just character. While we all make judgments as a reasonable part of living, those judgments should be righteous. It is not likely that a person who makes judgments *for a living* and is a person of corrupt living will make righteous judgments in the case of others.

This close correspondence between the "judging" that people do socially and that religious leaders did ecclesiastically, and the "judging" that goes on in court is more than merely coincidental in the Bible. Religious leaders *were* judges; it was part of their duty as outlined in the Old Testament. The character of priests *was* the character of judges. So when Jesus told the religious leaders, "Judge not, that ye be not judged" (Matthew 7:1), it was particularly applicable.

He did not mean, however, that either priests, judges, or anyone else should forego the act of "judging" altogether. People whose Bible knowledge is mostly casual or, shall we say, without much depth, often blithely quote Matthew 7:1 to fend off criticism or Christian gospel witness, as if any assessment of other people's behavior or spiritual condition were a violation of Jesus' teaching. But the Greek word for "judge," *krinō,* has different shades of meaning depending on context. In the context of Matthew 7, it means to criticize censoriously, to pigeonhole people with the intent of disregarding their importance. Jesus uttered the words, "Judge not," on several and probably many occasions; the reference from John 7, above, illustrates that, and it shows that he taught that people can and should make righteous, *just* judgments.

My family went to a local restaurant one day and was shown to a table by a hostess who made light conversation with me while someone gave the table a last wipe-down. She looked at my jacket, which bore the emblem of our state's Summary Court Judges Association, and she said, "Oh, you're a judge!" And then she said something to the effect that years ago she had thought she might be interested in being a judge, but that she was hesitant to go that way in life because, "You know, like Jesus said, 'Judge not.'"

I was smiling at her as she told her tale but I interrupted her at this point. "Well," I said, "that's not all he said. He also said, 'Judge righteous judgment.' He wasn't talking about whether or not there could rightly be human judges and courts. He was talking about mean and hypocritical judgment of other people, putting them in boxes and thinking little of them because of their faults—when we have perhaps worse faults of our own." She nodded and listened intently as I briefly put on my "pastor hat" and gave her a little scripture teaching, all while we waited for our table to be ready.

Then she said, "You see, I knew you had to be a good judge.

46

You just have that wise look." (She was talking about my gray beard!) I took the compliment humbly, just thankful for the brief opportunity to broaden someone's understanding of Jesus' teaching: the human judge, perhaps more than others, needs to be a just person, not hypocritical, not seen as a criminal himself when he passes sentence on criminals in court.

Scriptures describing the necessity of just character for the judge closely parallel those describing the priority of *doing* justice in the courtroom, as detailed in the previous chapter. But continuing to look at the person of the judge himself, the Bible addresses other character traits that exhibit themselves in his dealings with people in court. Among them is the quality of fairness.

The Judge Must Be Fair

The quality of fairness has long been associated with the best of rulers and judges:

If a king judges the poor with fairness, his throne will be established forever (Proverbs 29:14 NIV).

The Hebrew word translated "fairness" in the New International Version has the fundamental meaning of "truth." Contextually, it may be rendered differently. Older versions tend to have "truth," less older versions "faithfully," and newer versions "fairly." "Fair" means to be marked by impartiality and to conform to established rules, in one's dealings with other people.

Fairness is impartiality
The judge who is fair will not treat people differently because he has some kind of relationship with one and not the other, or because one is a person of note and the other is not, or because one is influential where the other is not, or because one has an attorney and the other does not.

The fair judge will not lean toward finding *for* one party because he likes that party's looks or speech or some cultural indications he prefers. He will not treat parties differently because of racial or ethnic factors. Unless a quality of a litigant or a defendant is specifically relevant to the case at hand, the fair judge will not consider it at all in his judgment or verdict.

Further, the fair judge will apply the established rules—the law and the rules of court—with equity. The same rules apply to all.

I had two litigants in my court for a civil suit in a landlord-tenant matter. The plaintiff-landlord happened to be a known figure in county politics, and at the same time a religious leader, a pastor of some kind—as I remember, not of a particular church. He was in my court that day with an attorney, a fact that had put the defendant, alone at his table, at some unease, as I could tell.

As Plaintiff's attorney began his case, his client on the stand, he began by asking the plaintiff about his work, his involvement in the county, and so on. Soon he would ask him about his religious leadership—I could see where this was going. It was more than an attempt to identify the plaintiff: he was trying to get away with eliciting blatant character testimony. According to rules of evidence, testimony about character is not admissible unless offered to rebut specific accusations. Just getting on the stand to begin with and telling the court how good a person you are, hoping that will make your case more believable, isn't allowed. Perhaps the attorney was not taking this tack hoping to influence me; he should have known that I wouldn't be so easily influenced. Perhaps he was more interested in overwhelming the defendant with how respected, how admired his client was, and hoping to intimidate him from the start.

The defendant didn't know about the rules of evidence and couldn't be expected to, and he didn't know to object. Since he did not have an attorney who would know and would object, I objected for him, and cut short the attorney's attempt to put his client in a parade of self adulation. If I remember correctly, I referenced Rule 404, giving him a definitive clue that I knew the rules of evidence, and implying with at least as much clearness that I, myself, wasn't going to be influenced by the plaintiff's towering stature in the county.

The case went pretty much by the book after that.

Fairness recommends the judge to the people

As a practical matter, disciplining himself or herself to be strictly fair recommends a judge to the community. People will learn by experience that a judge is fair, and they will trust the system to do justice. This doesn't mean that everyone who goes to court will get what he wants. It simply means that a court known to have a fair judge will be generally respected.

The Old Testament reflects the previously noted fact that religious rulers in some positions were judges, and it notes as well that the ultimate secular authority in the land, the king, also had the authority to act as judge. The Proverbs addressed this fact:

If a king judges the poor with fairness, his throne will be established forever (Proverbs 29:14 NIV).

The king was the supreme judge of the land. This was true in Israel, and it was also true in most political regimes. Remember that the Apostle Paul took advantage of that fact to escape the prejudicial judgment of Jewish authorities when he said, "I appeal to Caesar!" (Acts 25:11). The performance of the highest civil authority in a judicial capacity and his reputation of immanently fair decisions will greatly cement his position on the bench.

When I wore the robe, it was a common occurrence among magistrate judges for people who went through their courts and didn't think they'd gotten a fair shake to threaten the judge with reporting him to "his senator." During my service as a judge, other than my official duties I was essentially beholden to please a series of four senators, whose continued nomination of me was the fundamental determinant of my judicial longevity. If they didn't like me, I was out of a job.

49

The first three of these men had very short tenures due to death, illness, and other professional aspirations. The last was still serving in the senate after my retirement. When I informed him by letter of my upcoming retirement date, he responded with a letter of his own. Of most note to me was a one-sentence paragraph: "I have never had a complaint about you." That was a humbling and appreciated revelation.

As I noted in the Introduction, my predecessor served for thirty-nine years in his post, and throughout the time I served on the same bench I continued to hear "old-timers" remark how fair he had been. I was glad to occupy a post with a reputation for fairness and I intended to continue the honorable tradition.

Fairness must be affirmative

Sometimes judges must intervene or be proactive rather than simply reactive, to assure fairness, because it isn't just their own decisions that need to be fair, but also the shape of the proceedings in court themselves.

In the previous chapter I mentioned that magistrate court rules in South Carolina require the Summary Court judge to make certain that unrepresented litigants are able to present all relevant claims and defenses, to the extent of questioning them if necessary. An interesting Bible verse reflects a heavenly parallel:

You, Lord, took up my case; you redeemed my life (Lamentations 3:58 NIV).

The NIV reflects the legal context of the phrase and renders it in courtroom language. The verse depicts God's appropriation of two roles: advocate and judge. To transfer this Old Testament verse into a New Testament context, where the Trinity of God is fully revealed, we see that biblically God is both judge (as Father) and advocate (as Christ). Later in the New Testament, 1 John 2:1 specifically calls Jesus Christ our Advocate with the Father. Hebrews 7:25 further says, "He (Jesus) ever liveth to make intercession for them (the saints)."

In our country's justice system, not only does the three-branch system of government keep the executive (governors, president, etc.) and the legislative (congress, etc.) out of the role of the judiciary, but in the judiciary itself roles are separate. Attorneys take up and plead cases while judges hear and decide them.

In magistrate court, however, the exception for litigants without lawyers puts the judge in the position of looking like he's an advocate, when he finds himself having to question someone, as the rules may require. This can be a touchy matter for the judge. The last thing he wants is for the opposing side's attorney to appeal the judgment of the court on the basis of a claim that the judge showed bias in his questioning "parties and witnesses." More than once I turned to an attorney and put on the record a little impromptu speech about magistrate court rules, my understanding of the delicate line between judicial fairness and judicial advocacy, and my intention to question a witness only as much as necessary. Without exception, attorneys nodded. It wasn't their first rodeo.

What saves the judge when he has to assume the questioning role of an attorney is his rigorous training and practiced discipline. In fact, he may find it helpful if, going into a trial where he knows one or both parties lack representation (which in magistrate court is *usually*), he writes out questions he knows will not be construed as biased. But no fear of being thought biased should keep him from affirmatively probing the case of the litigant if it is evident that the party himself or herself doesn't know how to proceed.

I will add that I never had a lawyer object to my questioning when it became necessary, or appeal because I had done so. This was another reason for a "Whew!" when I finally left the bench for the last time.

The judge's personal, affirmative approach to fairness reflects the quest for justice of the court in general, as just described, and as taught in Proverbs 31:8-9. In either case, the model of the Bible lays on judges the charge to be not only fair, but wise.

The Judge Must Be Wise

The Bible's repeated command to judges was to be wise. An interesting example of this command is found in the writings of the scribe Ezra, who was among those who returned to the land of Israel after the Babylonian captivity. For months and several years as they were reestablishing the nation, though under Babylonian oversight, God revealed this imperative to Ezra:

And you, Ezra, according to God's wisdom that you possess, appoint magistrates and judges to judge all the people in the region west of the Euphrates who know the laws of your God and to teach anyone who does not know them (Ezra 7:25 CSB).

The process of selecting judges is included for Israel in this text, but in application to other political systems the prominent teaching is that whatever process is used should be considered the essence of wisdom. God's assessment of Ezra was that he himself possessed the wisdom, which came from God, to appoint magistrates and judges.

This one-man process was not unusual, either for nations in general or for Israel in particular. From the beginning, God's plan had been to mediate his leadership and rule of Israel through a key prophet to the regional judges and other officials. Long before, when Israel demanded that God give them a king, the current prophet and priest, Samuel, at God's instruction relented, but Samuel was still in the position of speaking prophetically to the king. With less and less righteous kings, to the point of having completely godless and wicked kings, Israel's entire "political" and therefore judicial structure broke down and injustice was rampant.

But after Israel's return to its land after captivity, God instructed Ezra essentially to go back to the original model, without a king, but with key prophetic figures again in leadership. The judges who would keep order in their respective regions were schooled in the law by this key prophetic figure, not now called either prophet or king, and they would themselves educate Israelite people in outlying areas in the laws of God.

The key point of this passage, however, is that the appointment process was inspired and directed by God, and under the political structure that had become a reality for Israel, his wisdom was incorporated in the selection of judges. These judges then became the examples and teachers of wisdom where they were sent to serve. *The judge must be wise.*

A great deal of thought accompanied by a high degree of education in the areas of philosophy, history, religion and political theory, went into the design of the American system of jurisprudence put together by our Founding Fathers. The systems in place in the states preceded the federal design, and accordingly they have variations. But again, the method is not the core issue: the wisdom of the process is in view, and the end of the process should be the selection of wise judges.

Summary Court judges aren't principally engaged in using their wisdom to teach, although they frequently have the opportunity to educate the public on the law. The window of the court's office is often the classroom for people who come wanting something to be set right and not having any idea how to go about it. And sometimes the courtroom is where the judge may want to impart some of his wisdom to litigants as part of his handling of a case or giving instructions to one or both parties.

But the necessity of a judge's possessing wisdom is most evident in his disposition of cases themselves, particularly where thorny issues have created a complex interrelationship of people, possessions and or expectations. A judge must plumb the depths of what wisdom he has, navigate these waters, avoid the minefields, and arrive at the port of a thoroughly just decision. Through the years, the really wise judge will know his wisdom must continue to deepen, and he will seek it at its ultimate source, the All Wise God.

Perhaps the penultimate example of wisdom not just in the

Bible but in all history was King Solomon, whose wisdom has become a byword and an icon everywhere. The wisdom of Solomon was exhibited early in his reign when he heard the case of two prostitutes who lived in the same house and had newborn babies. In the night, one sleeping mother rolled over on her baby and smothered him accidentally. She discovered it before morning and switched the two infants while her friend was still asleep. In the morning they argued over which baby was which, and they came to the king about it.

Solomon's wisdom was an instant classic. He called for a sword and announced that he would divide the surviving child and give half to each woman. Instantly one of the women said she gave up her rights to the child—Give him to the other woman, she said, but let him live. The other woman, I believe, knew she wouldn't be able to live with the guilt, and she said, No, give us each a half! Solomon rendered his decision succinctly:

"Give the living baby to the first woman. By no means should you kill him; she is his mother" (1 Kings 3:27 NIV).

When my judge friend first contacted me years ago about my possible interest in taking his bench, once I agreed, he had me come to his chambers for an afternoon or two of what one would have to call judicial training. Irrespective of what the Court Administration would tell me, of the training I would receive at the Judicial Academy, and prior to any of these official sessions, the judge just wanted to talk about his long experience and tell me not just about the tasks of the office and such, but also about his philosophy of justice. Two things stand out in my memory as representing much of what he said by way of illustration.

One was that often the decision of the judge involves splitting the baby. I knew what he was talking about, but it was curious that he used the phrase as it has evolved in legal circles and elsewhere. That form of the phrase does not, in fact, reflect what happened in Solomon's court. No baby was split. It was only threatened. But what the phrase has come to mean is often that a judge might come to a decision to give a plaintiff, for instance, part of what he wants but not all of it, thereby placating both parties, *somewhat.* In my experience, that rarely happened. I *never* adopted it as a strategy just to placate one or the other party. I did occasionally find that the evidence supported one of several claims but not another, and my decision (almost always fully in writing) detailed those findings and justified the lesser amount of the reward sought. But from the first, I was leery of the idea of responding to my own uncertainty by almost arbitrarily doling out half-victories to each side.

Nor do I actually think that's what my friend meant. I think he just meant that sometimes disagreements were so complex or evidence so scant for either side that the decision I would render would wind up containing concessions to both sides, with someone's being the technically prevailing party.

The other thing my judge friend said that I remembered long after was that most civil actions in magistrate court are just disagreements between two honest people about money. The part about money is conspicuously obvious, but the description of the two contestants as both being honest was memorable. And I found it to be true, overwhelmingly.

Yes, there were times when one of the people before me was a crook who just hadn't been caught yet at something actionable. I think of a particular car dealer who was of eastern European extraction and who I believe was engaged in something that went well beyond the particulars of his car business.

But most of the time I saw parties each of whom honestly believed they were due to get, or keep, an amount of money. They believed they had acted honestly in regard to the other party. They didn't see themselves as trying to cheat anyone. They just didn't agree with each other. And that was what called for Solomonic wisdom: to sort through the evidence, go strictly by the law, and make an unassailable decision.

What's really interesting is that in the process of approaching cases like this, every once in a while I had both parties thank me for my decision. Now, sometimes both parties—usually their attorneys—will thank the judge as a matter of courtesy when the losing party is actually thinking the judge is wrong, he's terrible, this was *so* unjust, and I'm going to appeal all the way to the Supreme Court. But some of my experiences were different. I had a defendant once in a civil matter who lost his case entirely, and who wrote me a letter in the week after the trial. He expressed his appreciation of what was his first experience in a courtroom, and he thanked me genuinely for making "the right decision."

I filed that letter with my keepsakes of the career.

Sometimes the wisdom the judge needs is one that takes in both the small picture and the big one, the individual case and its larger perspective.

These are the things that ye shall do; Speak ye every man the truth to his neighbour; execute the judgment of truth and peace in your gates (Zechariah 8:16).

In the original Hebrew of this verse, the phrasing has led to various translations. The NIV renders the last phrase, "render true and sound judgment in your courts." The Christian Standard Bible says, "make true and sound decisions within your gates." But interestingly, the Contemporary English Version translates it this way: "in court you must give fair decisions that lead to peace." That version follows the same idea as in the Amplified Bible, completed by Zondervan in 1965. The Amplified has, "pronounce the judgment that brings peace in [the courts at] your gates." This translation is faithful to the grammatical construction in the Hebrew. The meaning is therefore that decisions must be fair (KJV "truth") *and* must lead to, or bring, peace.

The reason for delving into the original language is to show that the verse instructs judges to see how their judgments in the immediate matters, which must be *just*—the small picture—should be informed, when necessary, by the interests of *peace*—the big

56

picture—in the community or populace at large.

This is not to suggest that the judge should make a decision wholly to keep a faction of the public from being outraged, or wholly as a conciliation to a faction, *regardless* of the judgment the evidence demands. It is to suggest, however, that what destroys a community's peace, what has upset them terribly in the way of crimes or civil injustices, must *inform* the judge, must have some bearing on, the judge's sense of what is just and fair in the first place.

This principle is of greater importance the higher the court a case is in, and greatest, perhaps, in the Supreme Court of the United States. Issues over which there is great outcry in the public beg to be adjudicated in such a way as to assuage that threatening outrage. If the genuine legal pathway to such a decision exists, the judge or justices are well advised to consider the virtual "advice" of the public.

This kind of public advice takes place in higher courts all the time in an official way, through friend-of-the-court briefs. A friend of the court is a person who has a strong interest in a matter that is the subject of a lawsuit in which he or she is not a party *(thefreedictionary.com)*. This party may file an *amicus curiae* brief , in which he or she (or they, or a corporation, etc.) will make an argument for the court's finding in agreement with them. Obviously parties on both sides of an issue may be allowed to file such briefs, and in allowing such the court is asking to be advised by the public what its thinking is, what its beliefs are. The wise court will be open to valid and persuasive arguments in coming to its own decisions.

The point is that wisdom is not proprietary to the individual. While we made the point above that the judge must be wise, his wisdom must not come entirely from himself. He must derive wisdom from a higher source, and Zechariah makes it clear that sometimes the community is a good reflector of divine wisdom—as good as the judge himself, or even better.

Americans are aware of various courts in the nation that have a reputation for rulings that are consistently representative of extreme elements of one political viewpoint. Accordingly, when they are appealed, they are usually overturned. This phenomenon is illustrative of the failure to be schooled by the larger beliefs of the public.

In smaller courts like mine, often the larger community would not even be aware of criminal or civil cases being tried. The newspapers don't carry articles about what's going on in the Summary Court or the Municipal Court (I was also a municipal court judge for my city). Outside the families and sometimes neighbors of litigants or defendants, most of the rest of the town and county was blissfully unaware of these cases, and to be truthful the issues in my court were not earthshaking.

But that doesn't mean that nobody cared what disposition I made of cases. Most of the time, the potential for peace or unrest due to a Summary Court decision came at the point of sentencing. When "guilty" verdicts were clearly called for by the evidence, there was no room for me to consider public sentiment. But when it came to sentencing, in most cases I had wide discretion. Where statutes did not include a mandatory sentence, I had wide latitude in sentencing—dollars or days—and even then I usually could suspend part or all of my own sentence.

Following the concept of being informed by the public, I usually asked for sentencing recommendations. In my criminal trials for county offenses, the State, represented by the assistant solicitor who had prosecuted the case in my court, would usually recommend the maximum, though not always. An occasional prosecutor would just defer to the wisdom of the court. Had I made a habit of giving the maximum sentence, it would have suggested that I never paid attention to the specifics or the nuances of the case or of the defendants. But if I became known for giving minimum sentences or suspending them entirely, it would have convinced people I was a pushover who didn't care about the effect of crime on the community.

Some of those "people" would be "the people," the State of

South Carolina, which didn't just prosecute individual crimes but which truly represented the people of the State, and truly wanted justice to prevail. I was well advised to consider the larger picture of the potential peace or unrest of the State over my judicial performance. While a Summary Court judge might be complained about by any miscellaneous citizen who went through his court, he might also be the subject of a complaint by the county solicitor. If the Court Administration were to get a complaint from the solicitor about a Summary Court judge, there might be a vacancy on that bench before long.

"Fair decisions *that lead to peace,*" is the instruction of scripture. The state, in choosing judges, must consider whether or not the candidate—or the sitting judge—is consistently convincing the people he serves that he is fair and just; for only in his doing so will he engender "peace" out in the community, insofar as his court's actions are relevant.

Above all, in following the charge and challenge to be wise, the judge should hear and consider this Bible principle:

The fear of the LORD is the beginning of wisdom, and knowledge of the Holy One is understanding (Proverbs 9:10).

In looking at the character of the judge, some references to classic stumbling stones must be made, and the Bible addresses the bench specifically:

The Judge Must Be Above Partiality

One of the chief sins of judges of all times has been that they are partial in their dealings and decisions. Moses addressed this issue when he gave Israel God's law:

Do not follow the crowd in doing wrong. When you give testimony in a lawsuit, do not pervert justice by

siding with the crowd, and do not show favoritism to a poor person in a lawsuit (Exodus 23:2-3).

It appears to be witnesses, not judges, who are the specific subjects of these admonitions. But if it is important for witnesses to avoid partiality, how much more important is it for the judge who considers those witnesses' testimony to then render judgments that are equally without partiality?

A judge who sides with the crowd participates with them in their wrong. Refer to the discussion above about being informed by public outrage, and notice that the Bible strikes a balance, saying that the judge should most certainly consider what sparks the moral outrage of his community, but that he shouldn't simply go along with the crowd no matter how morally corrupt their opinions might be.

What is most interesting about this verse is that Moses, speaking for God here, says that the court is not to be partial on the side of the poor anymore than the crowd. For justice to be done, guilt or liability must not be determined by the essentially irrelevant matter of how poor someone is, or how sick she's been.

What looks like an exception crops up in Proverbs 28:21, where Solomon wrote, "To show partiality is not good—yet a person will do wrong for a piece of bread." This idea is reflected elsewhere in the Bible and seems to suggest that if there were ever reason to be just a bit partial, to consider how poor someone is, for instance, when determining guilt, it would be that someone was so poor he had to steal to feed his family. That kind of ethical dilemma—a person has two choices before him where neither is morally right—certainly weighs heavily on the concept of justice, in court or not. Perhaps the solution for the judge, if this were the actual set of facts before him, would be in sentencing. But judges may justly dismiss charges where people were simply "up against a wall" and had no *right* choice to make.

The partiality the Bible enjoins, however, is not one based on the ethical dilemma faced by a poor person or any other kind of person, but rather partiality based on a class or some other descriptor irrelevant to the issues at hand.

Granted, witnesses for one side or another often do have valid reasons to be absolutely partial for or against a defendant, if they are victims of the crime charged, etc. But the court has rules against evidence being admitted consisting mostly of the opinion of a witness that the defendant "did it" when he isn't giving eye-witness testimony, for instance, but simply voicing his conclusion as if he were the judge.

Not everyone in court wants to abide by the rules, of course, and not everyone is above attempting to create partiality in the judge. Over the years, countless defendants in my court have attempted to persuade me to take their side emotionally, as if the evidence I was about to hear was far less important than their personal burdens in life. I wish had a nickel (or again, adjust for inflation) for every time a defendant began his case with, "I'm disabled, your honor."

Sometimes, since I offered even unrepresented parties the opportunity to give opening statements (if they knew what one was and wanted to give one), I would hear this "disabled" refrain when the trial had barely gotten underway. The odd thing is that almost no sign ever existed that the defendant was disabled in any way. I realize people may be disabled for medical reasons that aren't visibly detected, but you'd think that out of a thousand people who made disability a major component of their defense, at least a few of them would be self-evidently suffering from something physical that would validate the claim. In fact, I recall a case against a woman who had to be rolled into my courtroom on a gurney, who had to be cared for at home by the attendants who brought her, and who could move her limbs only barely. This was her permanent condition. Yet in her defense I heard not one peep out of her that she was disabled. She put most of those other defendants to shame, with their blatant attempts to lead the court to be partial.

The Bible is explicit in its command to avoid siding with

anyone on the basis of anything but evidence:

Do not pervert justice; do not show partiality to the poor or favoritism to the great, but judge your neighbor fairly (Leviticus 19:15 NIV).

The focus of this verse is on judicial decisions, but note that the people who come through the courts are "your neighbors."

In Summary Courts in South Carolina, much as with similar courts in every state, the magistrates who are the judges are the only representatives of the justice system in the State that most of the citizens in the community will ever see. Most citizens are not involved in felonious crimes and will never come before a circuit court, never be in the county jail, and never be in a state prison. Most citizens will never need a lawyer for anything other than a will or the sale of a house. If they happen to have a traffic ticket, or need to file suit for a small debt, or are sued for a minor dispute over a contract or service work, they will see a local magistrate or a city judge. That may be their only contact with the system of justice that grinds away day after day in every state.

The State's way of managing that brief contact is to provide for small courts in every area, every city, every town, where the magistrate-judges who operate those courts are "of the people." That was the reason that I was required to live in the district from which my State Senator came. Not only did that give him a certain elective relationship to me, but also it meant that the people he served would be the people *I* served. As judge, I needed to come from the people I would serve. It was important for me to be someone the community considered one of its own, and for me to consider them my neighbors.

I grew up in the town where I was a judge. My career took me to Texas and to North Carolina, but when I came back into South Carolina and was eventually nominated to be a magistrate, I moved into the immediate vicinity of my court. My being part of the community helped ensure that I would see myself as part of them, and thus conduct myself above partiality to any one of them over another, even when the law had to be upheld against someone.

In trying to live by this motto of impartiality, one of the more difficult obstacles to overcome is a natural human tendency to see things through the lens of social class, educational level, or ethnic or racial identity. The Bible addresses this temptation:

Hear the disputes between your people and judge fairly, whether the case is between two Israelites or between an Israelite and a foreigner residing among you. Do not show partiality in judging; hear both small and great alike. Do not be afraid of anyone, for judgment belongs to God (Deuteronomy 1:16-17 NIV).

Along with the now familiar reminder not to show partiality, note the illustration that one party is an Israelite and the other a foreigner. (Many older versions have "alien.") The Hebrew original for "foreigner" is a word carrying the implication of a "foreigner living in your community" (CEV). The realities of citizenship, national borders, immigration and other issues that we commonly think of in connection with certain terms are not directly comparable to the setting of Israel in the wilderness of Sinai or even the Promised Land some 3,400 years ago. But this much is evident: God expected people charged with crimes or people having disputes with each other to get fair treatment before whatever judge would handle these matters, *without* any partiality over matters of nationality or even regional identity.

The judge's sensitivity to this duty of impartiality occasionally forces him to consciously disregard what may be difficult to ignore. In criminal cases, for instance, defendants are predominantly of lower economic status. And it is simply a fact, demonstrated by cold statistics, that the percentage of crimes committed by minorities is higher for their percentage in the population than for the majority. The judge must file the facts of social, economic or ethnic identities in the back of his mind and place in the forefront of his attention the facts of the case. He is not to let social class of any kind, whether economic, nationality, race or anything else, affect his judgment.

Conversely, however, he should not be afraid to find *for* someone just because the opposing side has influential lawyers or is the state. The instruction in Deuteronomy is to "not be afraid of anyone," including the powerful, because "judgment belongs to God." The sense of this reminder is that the judge isn't acting on his own; he is acting with authority that ultimately derives from God.

Occasionally the ever looming temptation of partiality puts the judge in danger of actually joining the side of wrongdoing:

It is not good to be partial to the wicked and so deprive the innocent of justice (Proverbs 18:5 NIV).

The proverb writer had in mind the dispensation of civil cases where someone tried to use the court to further his quest to get rich—for instance, to steal land by one of a number of fraudulent claims. Some Bible translations treat the two halves of the sentence as though they were separate possibilities. The NIV translation of this verse rightly connects the phrases so that the first is seen as the cause of the second: being partial to the wicked *results* in depriving the innocent of justice.

In practice, this means that the judge must be on the alert for "unclean hands." He cannot ignore the unethical or illegal things a plaintiff may have done even if the defendant might otherwise be liable.

Partiality can sneak up on anyone; judges aren't immune, and one can fail to realize how much favoritism has affected him. But in addition to the insidious tendency of human beings, including judges, to fall prey to partiality, the beast of bribery also threatens judicial character.

The Judge Must Be Beyond Bribery

The aforementioned Solomon commented on this problem among people in power:

A wicked man secretly takes a bribe to subvert the course of justice (Proverbs 17:23 HCSB, CSB).

Earlier in this chapter I commented on what I believe is an unfairly skewed image of judges as shown on television and in movies. It's the result of exaggeration, but that means there's something there to blow out of proportion in the first place. Bribery is a problem, not just in the judiciary but also with public officials of all kinds.

When I entered the office of magistrate, during my first few months I had several interesting and somewhat strange encounters the like of which never took place thereafter. A man came to my office one day who claimed to be the father of a young woman who would be facing the municipal judge (across the hall from me) in a week or so. He asked me if I would speak to the other judge and ask him to go light on his daughter. He didn't use the words, "go light." I don't remember what his circumlocution was, but that was the gist of it. And I recognized this for what it was—my ethics training was fresh on my mind—and without sounding condemnatory I told him I was bound by judicial ethics not to attempt to influence the decision of any other judge. Saying he hadn't exactly meant that I should do that, he backed off the request, and we finished our conversation with light chit chat, and he left. I never saw him again, and I don't believe anyone by the name he gave me actually existed.

Even more curious was the visit of a man who came to ask my advice about a matter between him and the county over easements. Someone had sent him a letter about removing a section of pipe he had installed, supposedly on county land. I told him I had no expertise in the matter, but he assured me that he just wanted advice on how to go about settling the matter with the county, and my being a county judge, and presumed to have some level of wisdom, suggested I might know how to go about it. I didn't see any danger in telling him if I were in his position I would call the person who had contacted him, arrange a meeting if necessary, and talk it out. By no means did I offer to contact the county official on his behalf, and in retrospect much, much later I thought he might have been fishing to see if I would.

My suggestion of making a contact himself seemed to me to be common sense advice, and I felt a bit foolish giving it. But he acted thankful and left shortly. A week or so later, he came back to the court to give me a gift. He said it was just a "thank you" for the advice, which he said had resulted in his being able to solve the problem with the county. I was obligated to deal with his "gift" and to indicate to him that I couldn't compromise my impartiality if he were ever to come before me in some matter. I thought he might be a landlord in the area. But I never saw him again.

There were several other visits or communiques that were odd, and it took a few months for me to look back on them and come to the conclusion that someone—I suspected the Court Administration, perhaps through the agency of the chief magistrate—had sent these people to test the new judge to see if he were easily bribed or corrupted in some other way. I never asked my friends at the Court Administration (and I became good friends with their chief attorney) whether they conducted such clandestine checks on new judges, and they might have denied such even if it were true.

I never shook the conviction that I had been tested, however, and I was certain that I had passed with flying colors. I'm not boasting; I'm stating the facts with an attitude of humility and thanks.

Bribery continued to be a problem in Israel through the period of the kings, and was one of the reasons judgment came on Israel:

...who acquit the guilty for a bribe, but deny justice to the innocent (Isaiah 5:23 NIV).

It is axiomatic, of course, that by accepting a bribe to give a verdict of acquittal, a judge denies justice to the victims of crimes. But "the innocent" in this verse does not refer to victims. There are two distinct bribes and their results here. Consider how the CEV renders the verse:

You accept bribes to let the guilty go free, and you cheat the innocent out of a fair trial.

In the first case, a bribe has been offered by a guilty person or his family or representatives, to secure a verdict of not guilty. In the second case, someone has bribed the judge or official to see to it that a person charged is found guilty, whether or not the evidence says that he is. In either case, injustice is done.

What is perhaps the most insidious characteristic of bribery is that it tends to become an accepted way of doing things among people in power—not just judges. It isn't as crass as someone in an alley handing off an envelope with cash and muttering about the agreed "fix." Instead, it goes by casual mottos, such as, You scratch my back and I'll scratch yours. Many people in politics and administrative positions of power apparently assume that reciprocation is simply the way things work in government, even to the point of accepting personal benefits. The legal system of lobbying at times is little more than bribery.

In Israel it was a frequent target of prophetic preaching:

Her leaders judge for a bribe, her priests teach for a price, and her prophets practice divination for money. Yet they lean upon the LORD, saying, "Is not the LORD among us? No disaster can come upon us" (Micah 3:11, BSB).

Usually it isn't just one group of people who are corrupt, but all of them.

The Judge Must Be Above Corruption

There is wide variety in the ways people can be corrupted. That goes for judges as much as anyone. Much of the time our hypocrisy consists of self righteous denial of one sin when we are guilty of something not substantially different. The Bible's admonitions are instead all-encompassing.

I also noticed that under the sun there is evil in the courtroom. Yes, even the courts of law are corrupt! (Ecclesiastes 3:16 NLT).

The by now familiar author Solomon penned these words, indicting his own officials who acted as judges. To him it simply illustrated how pervasive and inevitable corruption in all its forms was. For "courts of law" other versions have "place of righteousness" or "place of justice." These renderings are equally good and make the point that courts, above all places, should be places where righteousness shines and justice prevails. But sometimes courts are powerfully influenced by corrupt governments and judges do what will stand them in good stead with the powers that be, the powers that keep them on the bench.

He who justifies the wicked and he who condemns the righteous are both alike an abomination to the LORD (Proverbs 17:15 ESV).

The proverb presupposes that the judge knows very well that he setting a guilty person free or convicting an innocent person, but has secret or nefarious reasons for doing so.

But the proverb raises the issue of a judge's complete reversal of justice, now letting the guilty go free and now jailing the innocent. It prompts the question of what would lead a judge to behave in such a fashion. Certainly bribery could explain an instance or two. But what would explain a pervasive pattern?

Let's consider an unlikely, immensely exaggerated case: a being of completely evil nature, with nothing redeemable about him, would consistently act with injustice, even malice. This doesn't seem to be what is in view in the Old Testament when judicial corruption is condemned. Generally we don't see Mephistophelian characters in power. Instead, what appears to have been the problem in Israel, as it is everywhere in all times, is people bent in their morals and ethics by some kind of incentive, typically monetary. And that incentive seems to have been systemic.

The tip off to this being the case in Israel was Micah's saying that the officials operating in a system of bribery protested any warning that they were guilty of character flaws serious enough to warrant God's judgment: "Isn't the Lord among us? No disaster can come on us!" This sounds perilously close to corrupt politicians blithely singing, "God bless America," and thinking nothing of the inconsistency between their character and their claims.

Some other examples of corruption the Bible points out may be mostly the re-phrasing of what we've already seen:

It is certainly not good to fine an innocent person or to beat a noble for his honesty (Proverbs 17:25 CSB).

Why an innocent person would be fined is not explained, though the previous example in Isaiah 5:23 suggests that someone powerful wanted an innocent person out of his way.

An example of how innocent persons were sometimes punished simply because they had been charged or apprehended —before any tribunal determined any guilt on their part—is found in the New Testament in an account of Paul the Apostle. In the story beginning at Acts 22:23, Roman authorities stretched Paul out (with ropes, as on a rack) to flog him. He escaped only by telling them he was a Roman citizen—Roman citizens had rights that other people in subjugated nations did not have. Ancient justice was simply not up to the standards of western jurisprudence.

This kind of treatment by the Roman Empire was one of the reasons Jews chafed so much under its dominion. Yet before their Babylonian captivity, their own justice system had victimized the innocent when it suited the purposes of those in power. The extent of this kind of judicial and governmental behavior was such that the prophet Zephaniah called on the image of wild beasts to illustrate it:

> **The princes within her are roaring lions; her judges are wolves of the night, which leave nothing for the morning (Zephaniah 3:3 CSB).**

Avoiding all this partiality, bribery and all other kinds of corruption, the godly judge is to be one who imitates the Almighty in his righteousness:

> **…He will not judge by what he sees with his eyes, or decide by what he hears with his ears; but with righteousness he will judge the needy…(Isaiah 11:3-4 NIV).**

In this verse, the judge's not using his eyes or ears does not mean he doesn't look at the evidence or listen to testimony carefully; it means he doesn't let common factors by which people often misjudge other people affect his understanding of the truth and his reaching a true and just determination of a matter.

A judge's achieving the kind of character that puts him above partiality, beyond bribery and above corruption requires a quiver of godly attributes.

The Judge Must Be Selfless and Courageous

One of the main reasons a judge gets in trouble is the failure to abandon self-centeredness and learn to prioritize the good of the people.

Jesus' parable referred to above in Luke 18 made its point by telling a story about someone who was decidedly *not* selfless:

There was in a city a judge, which feared not God, neither regarded man (Luke 18:2 KJV).

The point Jesus made in this parable was that God was *nothing* like the unjust judge. God didn't have to be begged to give those who called on him in faith what they needed in the Holy Spirit.

The indictment of the unjust judge was both that he didn't have deep respect and awe of God and that he didn't put first the needs of the people he was supposed to be serving. He was in the position for himself.

Among judges, as with people who gravitate to other public positions, there are some with the attitude that the judiciary is a position of power and prestige offering the opportunity to make a good salary and make a name for oneself, and likely to be granted no end of personal benefits, concessions and honors. In other words, some people seek positions in the judiciary for the perquisites. They're there chiefly if not entirely for themselves.

No one is suggesting that a person who wants to be a judge must be entirely devoid of any motivation to make an honest living —judges get paid like anyone else for the services they render. The advisement of scripture is for candidates to search their own souls, and even more for those who select judges to vet these candidates, to see if they incline significantly toward the good of others over their own advancement. Are they civil servants? Or are they self-serving?

I have often said that despite the public's love of lawyer jokes, I have not experienced attorneys as deserving of the criticism as a class that they commonly get. In spite of that, I find well-devised lawyer jokes to be genuinely funny. My favorite is:

Q: Why do they bury lawyers ten feet under instead of six?
A: Because deep down, they're good people.

Perhaps I find that funny because I'm not a lawyer. Some Summary Court judges in my state are, but it isn't required. (Yet. Some moves have been made to require a law degree.) But even most lawyers appreciate a good joke.

Overwhelmingly, most lawyer jokes poke fun at their making tons of money. The charge of attorney avarice is proverbial.

I never had before me any attorneys with reputations of being slaves to the god of greed, I knew of a pair who eventually were distinguished by the goals they had in life.

They were two fellows who were partners in law. One lived in a grand, nearly palatial family home passed down to him by his lawyer forebears. Through friends who were judges, he became interested in the position of magistrate. Eventually a nomination came and he qualified and was sworn in. He continued to practice law part time while being a judge. Meanwhile, his partner carried most of the weight in the law office, and it began to be an issue for the partnership.

The lawyer-judge finally decided the salary of a magistrate wasn't as good as he could make if he pursued his law practice more vigorously, and he declined to be reappointed after his current term. Back at the law office, his partner made the opposite decision. He was doing very well as an attorney, but he accepted a nomination to be a magistrate-judge full time, leaving his practice of law as an attorney for good. He knew very well that the pay, while providing him with a reasonable and healthy income, was not what he could make as an attorney. It appealed to him for other reasons, including the inclination to serve his community.

But even if a judge is blessed with selfless character, there will come times when he is confronted with a threat that tempts him to compromise, or pressure that pushes him toward prejudice. Clearly the judge needs character traits for this moral combat:

Courageousness

A judge needs to be courageous. Even in the smallest of courts there will be times and situations when the judge senses that a decision he must make may make an enemy of someone or some force in the community that he would prefer not to alienate.

Why do you make me look at injustice? Why do you tolerate wrongdoing? Destruction and violence are before me; there is strife, and conflict abounds. Therefore the law is paralyzed, and justice never prevails (Habakkuk 1:3-4 NIV).

This is an important passage of scripture, in that it addresses the age old question of why God allows evil in the world. Habakkuk asks the question here and in v.13, and then phrases God's answers in 2:3 and 3:12, respectively. Habakkuk 2:3 essentially says that God says, "Wait for it." And Habakkuk 3:12-16 basically says, "Final judgment is coming."

Habakkuk says that in the long-suffering of God the "law is paralyzed and justice never prevails." As a modifier, "never" is hyperbole, but it certainly feels like it.

Faced with occasional instances of horrible violence or injustice, or just the ceaseless, persistent reality of crime, judges often wish they could bang their gavels and bring it all to an end— solve the problem of evil with one decisive verdict. It's in their blood.

They can't, of course. They can only hand out a few sentences here and there, perhaps giving a great sense of justice to a victim now and then. Neither can they make lawmakers write better or more godly laws —especially judges at the lower levels. They can only opine in their judgment and hope that their collective influence will make a difference for godliness, while they wait for the Almighty finally to bring down his own eternal gavel, when the last judgment comes.

But along the way one of my instructors in continuing judicial training said something interesting that encouraged me ever afterward. I wish I had written it down word for word at the time, but I didn't. It was something like this:

> "Your court, of course, is a Summary Court, not a court of record. You can't exactly set precedent that other courts would then have to follow. But you never know if a case will come before you where you have a question of constitutionality, and *you* may be the one whose judgment will set an example. You may get to speak a word that will be heard all the way up the chain to the top."

I left that training week inspired by the thought: It could happen. And it was one more reason that I continued to write out all my judgments, detailing my reasoning from the law, parsing it and every issue. Maybe somewhere along the way I might say something that would have repercussions beyond my little court, even after my time.

As a matter of fact, I learned from one of the staff of the clerk of court that when a winning party in my court carried in one of my written judgments to be recorded at the county courthouse, the staff there often passed the document around and read it. Hardly any magistrates, if any at all, wrote out judgments, as I did and as my predecessor had done. Perhaps the staff had read his judgments, too. I didn't know. And of course, I didn't know if they read my judgments for enlightenment or just entertainment. If they were just laughable documents, I don't want to know at this point.

The character of the judge is vital to the output of his court. Judges must be just, fair and wise, and keep themselves free of corruption. Where do judges get these qualities? If we summarize all these admirable and requisite qualities under the broad canopy of wisdom, then where does wisdom itself come from?

We turn now to answer that question.

Source of Judicial Wisdom

The documentary film "Planet of the Humans," by famed leftist Michael Moore, contains an interview with Kristin Zimmerman of General Motors during a press event about electric cars in Lansing, Michigan. The cadre of photographers and reporters watches representatives of GM and other organizations in a parking lot where one of the GM reps plugs a Chevy Volt into a charging station, saying, "It's as simple as that!"

Then an interviewer asks Zimmerman, "What's charging the batteries right now? What's the source of the…"

"Well, *here!,*" says Zimmerman, pointing to the building they've just exited. "It's coming from the building."

"I mean is it, um, what's their mix of power?" says the reporter.

"Oh," says Zimmerman, as if she had not thought of the concept before. "Actually, Lansing [Lansing Board of Water and Light] feeds the building."

"What's that?" asked the reporter, not understanding her completely.

"Lansing feeds power to the building," says Zimmerman.

"So, they're a…" says the reporter, trying to get her to talk about the source of the electricity itself.

"So, I don't know," she says, running her hand through her

hair and looking confused. "I betcha they're a bit of coal... oh! Lansing's heavy on natural gas, aren't they?" she says, still looking quizzical.

The camera switches to another interview, in the same parking lot, with J. Peter Lark, of the Lansing Board of Water and Light.

"Right now," asks the reporter, "the car's charging off your grid?"

"Right." says Lark, "What it would be charging off, uh, our grid which is ninety—about ninety-five percent coal."

Michael Moore's film intended to make a very different point. The official description of it says that the nation's leaders are "selling out the green movement to wealthy interests and corporate America." But in the midst of this film, which blames "global warming" mainly on human activities, is this gem of an interview. One of the almost giddy representatives of GM, convinced that her electric car is going to "save the planet," isn't even aware that almost all of the electricity that charges her car's batteries comes from the nearby coal-fired electric plant.

I've seen other interviews with people on the street who are in favor of electric cars and who have, not just an imprecise idea, but in fact *no idea* at all, that ultimately electricity in their batteries comes from power stations that mostly burn coal—some natural gas, and some nuclear. Electric cars are not being powered by "green energy."

In looking at the connection between the Bible and the bench, we've been considering: the ultimate source of justice, which is God; some biblical principles for the judiciary; and the Bible's description of the requisite character of a judge. On this latter subject, one aspect of character the judge needs is wisdom. It is my contention in this book—it is God's statement of truth in *his* book—that wisdom comes from God, *whether or not human beings realize it.*

One of the simplest statements of this truth is in the book of Proverbs:

The fear of the LORD is the beginning of wisdom, and knowledge of the Holy One is understanding (Proverbs 9:10 NIV).

The overall goal of the book of Proverbs is: "The beginning of wisdom is this: *get wisdom!*" (Proverb 4:7). And Solomon was not shy about repeating this goal and wisdom's source in the Lord.

Doubtless all judges everywhere are conscious of the need to be wise in order to do their jobs. They realize they serve in the role of judge because someone needs to know the law, be able to sort through facts, be able to understand issues, *be wise,* and render just decisions.

But just as obvious as this is the fact that not all judges everywhere are followers of the one true God, or believers in his written revelation, or committed to following his principles in their lives and their judicial roles. Where is their wisdom going to come from?

Here is where a major and vital principle of God's working in the world comes into play. At the very top of this discussion of the source of wisdom, we must look at the subject of the **general grace of God.**

This principle is also known as the "universal grace of God" and the doctrine of "common grace." They mean the same thing. I prefer the word "general." This is a thoroughly biblical doctrine, and it means that although man has become sinful in his every part, God has continued to be good to him in several ways: he continues to let the world operate as it was designed; he spares humanity the utter corruption of every thought and deed so that people can actually behave well toward each other; and he sees to it that whether or not they know him, leaders and governments can actually perceive the good and often use their authority for righteous purposes. The bottom line is that even those human beings who have no spiritual connection to their maker have a degree of ability to understand what good is and to behave that way.

This general grace of God is what explains that the human race did not destroy itself in depravity and violence within a very short time after man's rebellion and fall. It explains the divine strategy evident in what Paul said in Romans 13:1, that "there is no authority except that which is from God." It explains the principle Jesus was illustrating when he said in Matthew 5:45 that God "causes his sun to rise on the evil and the good, and sends rain on the righteous and the unrighteous." And this truth is encapsulated in another, wonderful way in the writing of James:

Whatever is good and perfect is a gift coming down to us from God our Father (James 1:17 NLT).

There is good in the world because there is *God* in the world. Now, we human beings *are not* basically good: we are basically sinful. But God has left, or God places, some good *in* us, so we will be able to live in relative peace with each other. These are the "good and perfect" gifts James refers to. God blesses us with beneficial thoughts and continues to lead us to do good, even though we may be completely unaware of his doing so, or indeed even though we may be people who completely reject the idea of his existence!

One of the most important qualities a person may possess and exhibit, wisdom, is among these gifts that come from God the Father. And while Solomon insists that the beginning of wisdom is to fear God, we may rightly detect that the wisdom of which he speaks is what we may call "godly wisdom," and that a level of wisdom that indeed *comes* from God can be attained in the world, and possessed even by those who are of uncertain beliefs about God, or who don't know of him at all.

If this were not true, then governments would be continual sources of utter chaos. Judges would be madmen. Fathers and mothers would be arbitrary sources of anything astute or enlightened for their children. The general grace of God provides for some level of wisdom to be acquired in the world so that humanity may not destroy itself while God's specific plan of the ages is being worked out.

On the basis of this general grace, then, we may say with full biblical authority that judges may be exhorted to learn wisdom. And we may say without hesitation that whatever wisdom they may gain and possess comes from God—whether they believe it or not. Just like the electricity in electric car batteries comes from traditional power plants, so whatever wisdom man has comes from God, even though he may not be aware of it.

By contrast, the person who has a spiritual relationship with his Creator and who possesses the Spirit of God within him, has access to a knowledge and wisdom that give him the potential to be much wiser than people who don't know God. In discussing this matter, the Apostle Paul drew a distinction between the "natural man" and the "spiritual man," and he said:

The person with the Spirit makes judgments about all things, but such a person is not subject to merely human judgments, for, "Who has known the mind of the Lord so as to instruct him?" But we have the mind of Christ (1 Corinthians 2:15-16 NIV).

Obviously, I made the connection of this verse to the subject of judges from that word "judgments" in v.15. Admittedly, the context of this verse is specifically about a person's ability to understand the gospel and the written word of God. It takes an act of God to bring a person to repent of sin and have faith in God through Jesus Christ. Then and only then can he begin to fully understand the Bible.

But in talking about our "judgments" Paul deliberately used the words "all things" in v.15 to make us aware that ultimately our understanding of the world and how everything relates to God and his plan is dependant on our knowing God and having his Spirit in us.

That understanding of the world includes human wisdom. For while human beings can attain some wisdom to function thoughtfully and peacefully in the world even without their knowing God, superior wisdom, the *wisdom of God,* depends on that knowledge. We may reasonably conclude, then, that godly character emanating from biblical faith is a superior qualification for judicial work:

A Godly Person Can Make a Great Judge

In another chapter we looked briefly at the fact that in ancient Israel, being a judge was one of the functions of priests. Two additional Bible passages make this point. The first is from the Old Testament:

> **In any dispute, the priests are to serve as judges and decide it according to my ordinances. They are to keep my laws and my decrees for all my appointed festivals, and they are to keep my Sabbaths holy (Ezekiel 44:24 NIV).**

Ezekiel's vision from God concerned the future of Israel's life after its captivity. As before, priests were to be judges. It was important for these men to be faithful in their priestly duties and their spiritual lives, so that they would be able to act with spiritual wisdom when they applied the ordinances of God to the range of issues before them in their "courts."

The prophets' (not just Ezekiel's) assessment of priests with regard to honor, honesty, morality, faithfulness to truth and law, etc., therefore applied equally to judges, meaning there is much prophetic material that judges in all times should pay attention to.

The second Bible passage referring obliquely to the judicial role of Israel's priests or leaders is from the New Testament:

> **...who through faith conquered kingdoms, administered justice, and gained what was promised (Hebrews 11:33 NIV).**

This verse is part of the "roll call of faith" as it is often called, a listing of groups or types of people in Old Testament times who lived out their faith in God and performed their various roles bravely, often sacrificially, so that eventually what God promised through his word would come about. "These were all commended for their faith, yet none of them received what had been promised" (Hebrews 11:39 NIV).

Note those who "administered justice." No clue is given as to who the author of Hebrews was thinking of at the moment. But a search of the Bible would give us multiple stories of leaders who, in the exercise of what we would call their judicial role, made decisions and carried out actions that called on them to employ divine wisdom. And it was that divinely attained wisdom that made them the caliber of judges they were.

This biblical truth, that godly people can become excellent judges, is illustrated in stories of God's chosen people, Israel, as they influenced the cultures and nations around them. Consider, for instance, Joseph, son of Jacob, whose envious brothers sold him into slavery to Midianites going to Egypt. Once there, he experienced some dramatic ups and downs but finally was recognized for his ability to interpret dreams. Pharaoh himself had a troubling dream and Joseph was called on to interpret it. He did so, giving the credit to God for giving the interpretation to him.

The dream was about a coming famine of seven years after seven years of plenty. Pharaoh had to prepare for these times. Joseph recommended Pharaoh look for "a discerning and wise man and put him in charge of the land of Egypt" (Genesis 41:33 NIV). The Bible then says:

The plan seemed good to Pharaoh and to all his officials. So Pharaoh asked them, "Can we find anyone like this man, one in whom is the spirit of God?" Then Pharaoh said to Joseph, "Since God has made all this known to you, there is no one so discerning and wise as you. You shall be in charge of

my palace, and all my people are to submit to your orders. Only with respect to the throne will I be greater than you" (Genesis 41:37-40 NIV).

No one would have dared to suggest that Pharaoh was not wise himself. Why didn't he take charge of this coming national crisis? Certainly he had wise men in his royal court as well. Why didn't he give this important job to one of them instead of a Hebrew who had recently been in prison?

He did it because his other advisors had shown themselves critically lacking. And though we are probably wise not to read too much into Pharaoh's statement that Joseph was a man in whom was the spirit of God—because as an Egyptian, Pharaoh was still a polytheist— nevertheless he did recognize in Joseph a divine knowledge and wisdom that was superior to members of his own royal court.

As second-in-command to Pharaoh, Joseph was extremely influential for the next fourteen years at the very least. And from what the scriptures say about his eventual encounter with his family when they came to Egypt from Canaan, it may be that he had judicial duties as well as economic ones:

Joseph was governor of the land, the person who sold grain to all its people (Genesis 42:6 NIV).

Remember that in ancient political systems high officials like governors were typically judges in their realms. In addition to his selling grain to citizens, apparently Joseph had judicial powers. When his brothers presented themselves before him to buy grain, he put them through a series of tests, accusing them of being spies, and threatening to have them executed if they didn't comply with his orders and prove themselves to be only what they said they were.

To their father, the brothers described this man they didn't know was their brother as "the man who is lord over the land." He had the power to make them be slaves (Genesis 44:10). And they were not exaggerating too much when they told their father, "In fact, he is ruler of all Egypt" (Genesis 45:26).

Remember that direct comparisons of 21st century jurisprudence in America, or in most countries, to civilizations more than 3,500 years ago is not advisable. Still, it is obvious that Joseph had what we would call judicial powers as part of his governance of Egypt under the Pharaoh. And the story makes clear that what qualified him for appointment and what made his performance so exemplary and so successful was his divinely acquired wisdom. As Pharaoh said, "There is no one so discerning and wise as you" (Genesis 41:39 NIV).

In addition to these Old Testament passages, an interesting passage from the pen of the Apostle Paul gives additional scriptural authority to the concept of a godly person's making a great judge:

When one of you has a complaint against another, how dare you go to court to settle the matter in front of wicked people. Why don't you settle it in front of God's holy people? Don't you know that God's people will judge the world? So if you're going to judge the world, aren't you capable of judging insignificant cases? (1 Corinthians 6:1-6 GWT).

This passage seems at first glance decidedly not to be about judges who are part of the governmental system. In fact, Paul was highly critical of the Corinthian Christians who were going to court with each other. A few verses after the ones quoted above Paul recommended they choose someone in the church to help them settle these disagreements. Basically, he was recommending arbitration with a church member as a mediator.

But the passage winds up making a supporting comment about Christians making great judges, since it says that God's people would be better at mediating than the world's people. Mediators do the job judges do in civil matters, just in a little less formal way, but parties still have to agree to abide by their decisions, if they don't come to a stalemate. Paul's discussion here makes the case that not only does it give a bad witness to the world that God's people take each other to court, but also Christians would make better judges in such matters in the first place.

By the way, the God's Word® Translation calls people outside the church, including secular judges, "wicked people." The KJV had "unjust," the NLT "secular court," and many other versions just "the unrighteous," all of which are a little less inflammatory. But Paul was trying to draw a sharp contrast between Christians and non-Christians to make his point.

Looking at the godly person's "toolbox of wisdom," among the most productive of his implements is communication with God:

A Praying Judge Will Be a Superior Judge

News in 2022 reported that a Texas judge who had earlier been enjoined from having vocal prayer at the beginning of his court sessions won a victory in the circuit court allowing him to resume these prayers as long as he opened them to other faiths and traditions. The judge was a former Pentecostal minister.

The prayer I have in mind that a judge should undertake is not public at all. It is private prayer. He should pray at home about the daily conduct of his work. He should pray in chambers as he deliberates and studies. And he should expect divine answers, because of what the Bible says:

> ...the LORD Almighty had said: "If you obey my laws and perform the duties I have assigned you, then you will continue to be in charge of my Temple and its courts, and I will hear your prayers, just as I hear the prayers of the angels who are in my presence (Zechariah 3:7 GNT).

In a vision from God, Zechariah saw a high priest named Joshua being anointed and garbed for service by God. An angel then mediated the word of God to Joshua, promising him his continuation in service and his special audience with God when he prayed.

The Good News Translation gets the gist of the last phrase in particular. The Hebrew is not obscure but is a bit vague. Translated literally it says, "And I will give you places to walk among these who stand here." Most translations have something like this, with the ESV saying, "I will give you the right of access among those who are standing here." The GNT takes this statement by an angel to be a reference to the other angels in God's presence, and for "a place to walk" the GNT gathers the meaning of perfect fellowship in prayer, since Joshua will serve on earth. Thus, its rendering, "I will hear your prayers (access) just as I hear the prayers of the angels (those) who are in my presence (standing here)." Translators who stick to the "word for word" concept don't allow themselves to go this far in interpreting as they translate, but I believe the GNT grasps what the passage means.

The promise this Bible verse makes to godly judges is that when they are faithful in living for God, then when they pray about their judicial decisions they will have a powerful connection to the Almighty, akin to the access that the angels themselves have to God. This is a remarkable and astounding Bible promise. A praying judge may be more likely than any other judge to render judgment aright, and it is likely that God enables him specially because his judgments affect the justice of the public, and potentially the nation.

At this point, the reader may think of the wide variety of court decisions making news since the turn of the 21st century, along with some decisions of great notoriety in the last quarter of the 20th. Some reversals have taken place, meaning that on some single issues major courts such as the Supreme Court of The United States have found first one way and then the other. On other issues, that court or another one has rendered decisions—often sharply divided—that have divided the nation as well. If nothing else the history of our major courts' decisions in this author's lifetime show that the courts are not unified in their view of the law.

The Bible speaks to the erring course of nations and their courts, in an ancient passage from Job:

When a land falls into the hands of the wicked, he [God] blindfolds its judges. If it is not he, then who is it? (Job 9:24 NIV).

This is a remarkable statement, as we shall see shortly. Its application gives us this truth:

As Goes the Nation's Wisdom, So Goes the Judges'

Job had already been discoursing about God as his Judge (v.15), whose actions in the world cannot be challenged because he is the ultimate justice (v.19). In this passage in chapter 9 Job is wondering aloud to his friends about God's sovereign control of men and nations, "wonders that cannot be fathomed" (v.10) and authority over everything. In the midst of this accounting of the hand of God over his creation Job inserts this observation about a "land falling into the hands of the wicked." What does he mean?

Obviously he could simply be thinking of lands around him where the people and their rulers have become extremely perverse. Job lived in the days of the patriarchs—he may have been either a contemporary of Abraham or have lived just before him. The land of Ur, from which Abram came, was a polytheistic place and certainly could have been quite wicked. Civilizations existed in all directions from where Job likely lived, including Egypt, which certainly could not have been described as godly from the standpoint of Job's own faith and what became Abraham's faith.

It is likely, however, that Job is referring to something else.

From Deuteronomy 32:8-9 we have Moses' divinely given interpretation of the events of Genesis 11, where God responded to the post-flood humanity's return to its religion of self-exaltation and abandonment of him. God's response was "giving the [other] nations their inheritance" (Deuteronomy 32:8). But he kept Israel as "the *Lord's* portion" (v.9 emphasis mine). Together with various other passages of scripture we learn that God allowed heavenly beings, called in some places "the sons of God" (Genesis 6:1, Job 1:6, 2:1), and other places "gods" (Psalm 82:1,5-6, John 10:35) or sons of the Most High (Psalm 82:6), to take administrative superintendence of the nations surrounding what would become Israel—the sons of Jacob, the grandson of Abraham.

It was clear that these heavenly beings associated with the other nations were (1) fallen from their created perfection, and (2) wanted to have a place of authority and power in God's creation. It was also clear about man that (1) "every imagination of the thoughts of his heart was only evil continually" (Genesis 6:5), and that (2) even after God started over with Noah, the generations after him returned to their willing ignorance of the Lord, the Creator God (Genesis 11:4). So God gave them into the manipulating powers of the "sons of God," heavenly beings (higher than angels) who have immense ability to influence the thoughts of human beings and direct them spiritually. (For another scripture passage about these beings, see Daniel 10:20-21). As Paul would later write:

And so God has given those people over to do the filthy things their hearts desire, and they do shameful things with each other. They exchange the truth about God for a lie; they worship and serve what God has created instead of the Creator himself, who is to be praised forever! (Romans 1:24 GNT).

This is what Job meant when he wrote about a land that "falls into the hands of the wicked." He was talking about the spiritual control of a nation or a culture.

I've gone into some detail about this underlying biblical teaching in order to make the point that God's way of working with Israel was *not* the way he worked out his purposes among all the other nations. Consequently, when Job commented about God's "blindfolding judges" when their nations had become wicked, he was saying that God didn't guarantee that judges would be able to remain wise in spite of the direction their culture was taking. Rather, as one might reasonably conclude, as goes the culture, so go the judges. As goes the nation's wisdom, so goes the judges' wisdom. As the nation increases its commitment to sinful principles and ideas, the judges who are part of that nation will become less and less wise, more and more committed to underwriting the nation's wickedness.

This order of events correlates with what we see in history. Courts do not lead the way into lawlessness; they reflect what people have become, what education has wrought, what foolish philosophies have done to political structures. Then, when judges have been put into place by people of corrupt ideologies, they reinforce what their electors have come to believe.

The reader can easily make his own application from his or her knowledge of history and current events. Even where courts have lingered in some semblance of wisdom as the nation erred, eventually judges believe the sinful ideas and lies that the culture taught them as they grew up in its communities and schools.

What is fascinating about Job's observation is his statement that in response to a nation's growing wickedness God "blindfolds its judges." What does this mean?

All of us are familiar with the image of Lady Justice. Little statuettes adorn law offices and court chambers throughout the country. The image is a representation of the Roman goddess Justicia. We judges and lawyers can wax eloquent about what it means that Justice is blindfolded. We explain that Justice must ignore the things the eye sees that tend to prejudice us in our judgments. We can't afford to see race, economic status, or anything else—just the facts!

Interestingly, Justice hasn't always been pictured this way. In fact, the Roman goddess Justicia, whose Greek parallel was Themis, was pictured as a young teenage girl who, yes, held scales to weigh matters, and sometimes bore a sword as a symbol of punishment, but who was quite wide-eyed and aware of everything.

In my 2011 book, *Lady Justice, International Icon,* I outlined the history of the addition of Justice's blindfold. Hans Gieng's 1543 statue on the Fountain of Justice in Berne, Switzerland is the earliest known depiction of Justice with a blindfold.

> The concept of a personification of justice as blind would have been foreign to the ancient world. In view of the fact that clear vision was a trait crucial to Themis and Justitia both, a blindfold would have made no sense to the Greeks or Romans. The accepted meaning of the blindfold since its appearance at the end of the fifteenth century has been the meting out of justice in an objective, impartial manner. …Yet even early illustrators of Justice blindfolded did not always intend the blindness to honor the judicial system. Some evidence suggests a few sculptors and painters saw judges as willingly blind to abuse of the law (*Lady Justice, International Icon, pp.13-14*).

Clearly, the reference in Job to God's "blindfolding" judges is not any kind of compliment, and is obviously not a reference to their impartiality. This symbolism for that quality would wait another 3,000 years or more to be invented.

Rather, what Job was communicating was God's rendering judges entirely blind to truth and righteousness.

Let's do a little study of the original language of Job. In the Hebrew, Job 9:23 begins with the word "If" or "when" —the translation of the Hebrew *imoso.* Then in 9:24, the initial "When" is picked up from v.23, as if the two couplets are both composed of a condition and a consequence. The verse is saying that God's response to the descent of a land into the control of wicked people in their wicked thinking is to see to it that their judges—who ought to be the ones who would put a stop to wicked laws and government administration—instead are somehow unable to see what's right and what is very clearly wrong. They are blindfolded to the truth.

In Hebrew, the words translated in the NIV as "he blindfolds its judges" may be literally rendered, "He covers the faces of its judges." Some translations basically render the clause that way while others actually say, "He blinds its judges." The NIV, like the CSV, Holman, BSB and others, says, "blindfolds," not meaning to suggest the modern, positive sense of the blindfold on Lady Justice, but meaning that the judges themselves have been rendered unable to see what's right: God's truth.

Again, this condition of judges is due to the previous and causative descent of their nations into dark, perverted sinfulness: wickedness. The Hebrew in v.24 for "wicked" is *rasa,* which often has the implied meaning of "the wicked *one,*" which would be Satan or another wicked being. This would underwrite the interpretation above, that nations are manipulated by fallen spiritual beings.

Are judges the last bastion of truth? When the court goes, is that a sign of the end? If God cuts off judges from wisdom, is the nation finished?

Possibly the message of later prophets in Israel gave a promise of hope, dependant on a nation's turning to godly principles and laws.

Where God Prevails Judges are Just

The message of the prophets to return to God is first and foremost a specific message to a specific people, Israel, in the context of their history. Yet since the coming of Christ the message of the Old Testament has never been considered to be so proprietary that it did not offer general principles of righteousness, revival and blessing to other people whom God invites to belong specially to him. For instance, Christians find particularly sacred and powerful the promise of 2 Chronicles 7:14: "If my people, who are called by my name, humble themselves, and pray and seek my face and turn from their wicked ways, then I will hear from heaven and will forgive their sin and heal their land" (NIV). When this text was written, "my people" referred to Israel. However, in Christian theology Jesus Christ "disarmed the powers and authorities"—a reference to those "sons of God" who previously were "in charge" (so to speak) of the other nations, and opened the way through the gospel for anyone, from any land, from any culture, to join "my people." Because of this fulfillment of the Old Testament's predictions of a Messiah, the principles of the promises given to Israel now apply broadly.

It is in this sense that The United States of America, more than any place in any time previous, is under the divine scrutiny that expects adherence to biblical principles and truth, and also metes out discipline for its departure from the same. For although the founders of The United States did not set up her government as a theocracy, there is no doubt that it is founded on the truths that emanate from the word of God. Even more than the principles that came out of the Enlightenment, the principles that emerged from the Protestant Reformation and then the First Great Awakening shaped the formation of The United States.

In this book I join thousands of others before me and contemporary with me in seeing the Old Testament's call to repentance, its demands of righteousness, and its promises about blessing in revival, as applying in their core principles to The United States of America, even more than to any other nation. Among those Old Testament scriptures are two messages from Isaiah:

The ruthless will vanish, the mockers will disappear, and all who have an eye for evil will be cut

down—those who with a word make someone out to be guilty, who ensnare the defender in court and with false testimony deprive the innocent of justice (Isaiah 29:20-21 NIV).

Isaiah foresaw the return of Israel to the promised land and the return of knowledge and worship of the Lord. The result would be that those who perverted even the courts of the land, would be done away with. That would include unjust judges, unbelieving judges, perverse judges, and judges who have conceded the modern godless values and allied themselves with its perversity. Yes, the hope of the courts is the spiritual revival of the nation's godly people.

A second word from Isaiah underscores the point:

On that day the LORD of Hosts will become ...a spirit of justice to the one who sits in judgment... (Isaiah 28:6 HCSB).

Isaiah says simply that where God prevails, judges are just. Just as where the nation became perverse, eventually the judges did, too, so when the nation is swayed toward godliness by the fervent spiritual renewal of God's people, the courts will reflect this renewal of justice and truth.

The source of judicial wisdom, as is my assertion in this chapter, is the one and only God, the LORD revealed in the Bible in its Old and New Testaments, the Creator of heaven and earth. Where masses of people honor and worship him and where their governments are greatly influenced by their convictions and holy living, judges will be more and more attuned to divine wisdom. Judges who believe in the One true and living God and who have a spiritual relationship with him through faith in Jesus Christ will have an even deeper understanding of wisdom and a special connection to God's just leading through the avenue of prayer.

Based on the biblical principles of the judiciary, the Bible's teaching about the character of good judges, and the source of wisdom itself, the scripture also offers some more finely focused advice to judges. These pieces of biblical advice take on a remarkably current common sense.

Advice to the Judge

Biblical advice, to one who believes in the divine authority of the Bible, is more than mere advice. It carries the weight of commandment, except where it is offered explicitly *as* advice, such as in some of the Proverbs. That said, even people not committed to Judaism or Christianity as a faith can usually recognize excellent advice in Bible teachings.

In fact, the Bible gives advice about advice! It says:

For lack of guidance a nation falls, but victory is won through many advisers (Proverbs 11:14 NIV).

The way of a fool is right in his own eyes, but a wise man listens to advice (Proverbs 12:15 ESV).

If any of you lacks wisdom, let him ask God, who gives generously to all without reproach, and it will be given him (James 1:5).

In the spirit of that last directive from the New Testament, let's discover what pieces of advice the Bible gives to judges who accept the goal and quest to pursue justice and justice alone.

Don't Rush to Judgment

Rush to Judgment was the title of a 1967 book by lawyer Mark Lane about the haste of the Warren Commission to blame the assassination of President John F. Kennedy on Lee Harvey Oswald alone. Lane borrowed the phrase "rush to judgment" from what Lord Chancellor Thomas Erskine (1788-1870) said in his defense of James Hadfield, accused of attempting to assassinate King George III. Erskine said:

> An attack upon the king is considered to be parricide against the state, and the jury and witnesses, and even the judges, are the children. It is fit, on that account, that there should be a solemn pause before we rush to judgment.

If it seems, upon technical analysis, that Erskine didn't exactly say, '*Don't* rush to judgment,' but instead, 'Pause a moment, and *then* rush to judgment,' we won't over-analyze him. Undoubtedly he meant that one should *never* rush to judgment, if rushing means shortcutting the process of full information and thorough deliberation. After all, the judge's oath (in S.C.) says:

> I pledge to listen courteously…and rule after careful and considerate deliberation.

Between those phrases, where I put an ellipsis, is the phrase, "act promptly." The judge in a Summary Court isn't to sit on all the evidence and testimony and his own cogitations on the matter and fail to give the parties a decision in a timely fashion. It's a *summary* court after all.

Nevertheless, the judge should not *rush* to judgment. "Careful" means taking the time and every other measure necessary to understand everything there is to know about the case as presented at trial and anything else in the record.

Our by-now-familiar source of biblical wisdom, King Solomon, commented on overeager judgment:

In a lawsuit the first to speak seems right, until someone comes forward and cross-examines (Proverbs 18:17 NIV).

Anyone, especially any judge, recognizes this as an almost too-obvious piece of advice. In fact, it's for just such a tendency of juries to reach a conclusion after a strong presentation by the prosecution that defense lawyers often try to avoid leaving a jury to think about the state's case over a weekend or even overnight, for fear that their first impression will never leave them. Instead, the defense often wants to launch into its case right on the heels of the prosecution, to balance out the impact of the evidence right away.

Judges aren't immune to first impressions, either. For this reason, obvious advice is still vital advice: don't jump to conclusions. Don't rush to judgment. Train yourself to listen first and decide later.

I once had a Summons and Complaint lawsuit where the two men who came *pro se* to trial were both ESL—English as a second language. One was German and the other Polish. They didn't need translators, but it was difficult to understand a word or two here and there. It was one of those trials where there was a great deal of evidence; it had to do with a major grading and landscaping project. When both parties had finished their presentations, there were a number of documents to review and lengthy testimony —about two hours of it—for me to consider. Some of the testimony I needed to hear again because I really hadn't been able to hear it well enough to understand every word of it the first time.

I thought I could see who was going to prevail from what the evidence presented, but it was one of those cases where, just to make sure, I announced that I would take the matter under advisement and rule within the week. Besides, it was quittin' time, and supper was waiting at the house.

I carried a copy of the bench recording home with me and listened to it that evening. Loading it into audio software, I plowed through the entire two hours again, increasing the gain on the volume by several times in places. Lo and behold, there was a portion of one bit of testimony I had not heard before as clearly as I thought I had. And though I thought at the time it was nothing significant, it turned out to be the linchpin of the entire case. Had I "rushed to judgment," even though I didn't think I would have been doing so, I would have rendered a verdict that was unjust.

In the verse above, not only does the proverb writer speak of first impressions, but he also implies that the first party to speak will likely do his best to cast his side of the story in the best light, leaving out any culpability or possibility of error on his part. In the case of the trial I just described, the parties had no attorneys, and I didn't get the feeling that either of them was doing anything more than giving his recollection and viewpoint. In cases where there are lawyers, while they are duty bound not to perpetrate fraud upon the court, that doesn't mean they don't "spin" the story to cast their clients in the most favorable light, and they do. The judge's oath, to "...rule after careful and considerate deliberation," is partly about taking the time to allow initial impressions to subside. Only if they re-assert themselves after thorough reevaluation should they be followed.

This is not to say that a judge should be paralyzed by fear of making an errant decision, by "over-thinking" a case. Seasoned judges don't have much problem with this, but greenhorns may encounter it. I remember well the first case I tried, in "the early days," where after hearing both sides I retired to deliberate, mostly because I had no clue who I was going to find for. In chambers, I weighed the evidence and weighed it again, looking up now and then at my 16" figurine of Lady Justice, her scales frustratingly in balance, giving me no clue. What if I got it wrong?

I did finally go back in and render a verdict, and it was the right one. And things quickly got better from there. If they hadn't, I would have decided I was in the wrong profession.

There are probably many other "don'ts" that would make good advice. Consider some of the "do's" that the Bible recommends as well.

Be Neither Too Lenient Nor Too Severe

One of my favorite novelists has a detective character who frequently must see a judge about a search warrant. Almost invariably, the character's thinking is how one judge is a "no-go" if the probable cause for the warrant is thin, but how another judge is her "go to" judge in such cases, because he is more interested in her as a woman than the particulars of the warrant. Guess which one she usually goes to.

Judges can also get the reputation of being either "hanging judges" or pushovers, if their handling of criminal cases—particularly sentencing—tends to be too hard or too soft. The Bible speaks to that issue, where God tells Israel through a prophet:

> **…I won't make an end of you! I'll discipline you justly, but I'll certainly not leave you unpunished (Jeremiah 46:28 ISV).**

The version of this verse I selected makes clear the alternatives available to God in punishing Israel for its generations of continuing and worsening idolatry, immorality and folly. He *could* make an end of them entirely, but he won't. On the other hand, he *could* let them go unpunished, but he won't do that, either. He will discipline them justly.

What God was saying through the prophet was not exactly that he would take a middle course, as if averaging out the alternatives were in any sense the definition of justice. Instead, he was saying that justice lay neither in being as severe in his dealing with them as he could be nor in being as lenient as was possible—doing nothing. Justice consisted of factoring in his purposes: his ancient choice of them as a people; his promise to Abraham; his promise to David; his longsuffering with them that he didn't intend to be wasted; and his messianic plans. If he destroyed Israel, all his plans were destroyed as well. If he just let them go, he would not be just, because their sin needed punishment.

The Hebrew *mispat* in Jeremiah 46:28 is rendered in some other versions as "fair" or "appropriately" or even "in measure." I believe the ISV correctly translates it "justly." Applying this verse to human judges, the judge is to discipline with justice, tempered with mercy where appropriate, but not failing to punish where needed. Be neither too lenient nor too severe.

The importance of following this advice is explained further in another biblical advisement, which we might see as a corollary to the previous one.

Sentence to Deter, Not Demoralize

Most statutes include specific sentences, or a range thereof, for defendants found guilty. In Summary Court in South Carolina, if a sentence isn't laid out in black and white in the law, it's presumed to be thirty days in jail or a five hundred dollar fine, plus costs. Most bonds are set at the amount of money that would be owed in fines *if* the defendant were to be convicted, so that if the defendant doesn't show for trial, the bond can simply be estreated —exacted from the bail posted, to pay the fine. It's easy for the magistrate judge to just "go with the max" on fines. She may even think that sentencing everyone to the same fine gives the impression of being even handed, as if she weren't showing favoritism.

But spitting out the same figure for every defendant doesn't so much say that a judge is being even handed as that he or she is being an automaton. People's situations vary. What is an easy payment of $500 for one person may be a major hit to his family for another. And the result of giving the same sentence to all may in fact be that some get off so easily they aren't afraid to go out and do whatever it was they did, again! Meanwhile, another needs to arrange to make time payments on his fine, and each of those payments my grind him down to the point that he actually considers other criminal activity to get money to live on.

The first part of Proverbs 19:25 is especially applicable to judges. The purposes of lawful sentences are several, including punishment—to teach the lawbreaker a lesson. The goal should be for the lesson to be learned without going so far as to embitter. Wise discretion of the judge is called for.

A popular channel on YouTube is "Caught in Providence," featuring misdemeanor court appearances before Judge Frank Caprio. Caprio is a fascinating study in homespun wisdom and hometown friendliness. Every now and then he throws the book at someone, metaphorically speaking. But then again, he'll question someone about their income, living conditions, etc., and he'll set a fine very low and perhaps suspend even that. People frequently cry with relief in his courtroom because he showed mercy where it was greatly needed. Probably the videos are weighted toward his more compassionate dealings with the wide variety of people caught breaking the law in Providence, Rhode Island. But these entertaining snippets from Judge Caprio's courtroom are very illustrative of the concept of sentencing to deter, not demoralize.

In my years of adjudicating cases of fraudulent check charges, most of the defendants who came before me had records of having written bad checks four or five times previously. The evidence in these cases, as I described earlier in this book, had to constitute a prima facie case even for the county to get a warrant. So except for that rare case where some surprise evidence by the defendant put a speed bump in the state's case, these cases would end with, "I find you guilty as charged; sentence is a fine of $500 and an order to make restitution."

But sandwiching these typical cases were the case of a first-time offender, on the one hand, and the case of someone who had written several dozen bad checks over the years—or even more.

I sentenced a man who had never written a bad check before to make restitution (only about $100) and told him if he showed proof of restitution within ten days, I would suspend a fine of $75. He complied, and I never saw him again. In this case, he had risked the timing of his check and had technically broken the law, but my sense of him was that he wouldn't do it again—I don't think he had ever been charged with a crime before and he was well into his sixties.

By contrast, I had a woman before me who had written about three dozen bad checks over a period of two years, just not any in my jurisdiction. She spun some story about how it was all some sort of mistake, but she couldn't contradict the evidence against her. And the fact that she had had several months to respond to the letters the County Solicitor sent her from the Worthless Check Program, but had not paid up, told me she was just hoping it would all go away without her having to pay for her fraud. I found her guilty and ordered her to show proof of restitution by a certain date. And then she would owe a fine of $500 plus costs, or spend thirty days in jail. That's the maximum. She didn't show proof by the date I gave her. She didn't pay the fine. I subsequently signed a warrant for her arrest, and she wound up touring the county jail for a month. I don't recall seeing her before me again, so perhaps the sentence did, in fact, deter her. Or maybe she just made certain to write her fraudulent checks in another county.

Stories of defendants who appear multiple times on identical charges certainly suggest that such people likely have little regard for the law. Due to my upbringing, I find this kind of mentality hard to understand. Not everyone was raised with the kind of respect for authority that I was. But should a judge make concessions for people's upbringing? Or should he sentence with the goal of changing people's course of life, even when they're old enough that it probably won't do any good? It's a challenge to the judge's philosophy of sentencing, and it brings up another piece of advice that comes from scriptural principles:

Find Contempt When It's Theirs, Not Yours

As addressed briefly in the first chapter, contempt of court is something judges need to treat seriously. God gave Moses the principles for dealing with this misbehavior:

Anyone who shows contempt for the judge or for the priest who stands ministering there to the Lord your God is to be put to death (Deuteronomy 17:12 NIV).

Some explanation is obviously due here! Moses led an otherwise theocratic nation. That, and any number of other cultic and sociological factors explain the drastic difference in the penalty for "contempt of court" between ancient Israel and any modern country. We have no idea what demonstrations of contempt for judges or priests may have taken place among Israelites in those very early days. I suspect they were more than a scoffing word here or there. That said, the penalty prescribed was intended to cast in the most serious kind of light an attitude of disrespect for the authority of God mediated through his chosen leaders.

The typical penalty in a Summary Court is thirty days in jail for "direct" contempt, where the contempt is shown before the judge in court. There's also "constructive" contempt, which is, for instance, failure to comply with a court order, such as making restitution.

Consider the judge holding court, when a defendant says or does something that presents itself as possibly meriting a finding of contempt. A relevant question for the judge is to determine whether what he feels at the moment is a genuine protectiveness of the dignity of the court itself, or more a feeling of contempt of his own for the defendant, who may have made a decidedly negative impression on him throughout the trial so far. Is the judge defending the court or exhibiting his own hostility?

I saw a training film once where a defendant said something dismissive about the judge or the proceedings and the judge calmly announced that the defendant would spend the next thirty days in jail for contempt. When the defendant heard the judge say this, she uttered a profanity, and he added another thirty days for contempt. When he did that, and as she was being led out of court, she said something else undecipherable, and the judge calmly added yet *another* thirty days. It wasn't clear from the video what her actual crime had been, but the point of the video was for judges to debate whether or not it appeared that the contempt citations were justified.

Even in cases of constructive contempt, there are rules aimed at keeping mere emotions out of things. When I first began conducting fraudulent check hearings, the long established practice was for failure to make restitution and/or pay the fine to be followed automatically by an arrest and commitment to the county jail. The defendant would then be brought over to the court to answer for his failures. Somewhere along the line a new state supreme court justice issued an order making sure that magistrate courts were complying with court rules about contempt charges. Before an offender who hadn't complied with an order could be jailed, he had to be brought into court on a "Rule to Show Cause," which had to be served by a constable or deputy. He then had to come to court, explain why he had not complied, possibly be given another time period to comply, and so on.

There were two typical results of this procedure. First, the person was difficult to serve with the "Rule to Show Cause," and second, when served, he might not appear to "show cause" why he should not be jailed for contempt. And even if he showed up for a hearing and was given another thirty days or so to comply, typically he didn't, and the merry-go-round continued.

The rules are the rules, but it certainly gave convicted offenders plenty of opportunity to show their contempt of the system. And the rules exist at least in part to protect the judge from himself. An abiding sense of authority attends the mere fact of being a judge, and an intoxicating awareness of power lurks in the exercise of contempt findings. Rules establishing a measured process of dealing with contempt situations help quell the misuse of that power.

As for situations of direct contempt, perhaps it is the very nature of Summary Court charges— misdemeanors—that makes for less tension between judge and defendant, which in turn keeps situations of contemptuous behavior to a minimum. At any rate, a judge who is committed to growing in wisdom and getting ever better in acting justly will train himself to recognize when he is being tempted to overreact. To adapt an old saying, make sure when you're baring your heart you're not just venting your spleen.

Turning again to the civil side of the court's business, another piece of advice stands more as a challenge to the lofty goal of the judiciary:

Don't Be an Agent of Exploitation

One of the constant concerns of godly kings as well as Old Testament prophets was the tendency of the society as it developed to victimize the poor. Jesus' saying later to the disciples, "The poor you always have with you," was an observation of the perpetuation of the underclass by virtue of the very evolution of economic and political systems.

While in Old Testament times, as today, some people contributed greatly to their being poor by refusal to work, it was more often true that disease impoverished some, lack of opportunity to train for professions hobbled others, and merely being born into a family that was poor put still others at a disadvantage. It would be grossly unfair to make direct comparisons of ancient civilizations to the United States in the 21st century, but some very general principles do make the lessons of old applicable to today.

Do not rob the poor because he is poor [and defenseless], Nor crush the afflicted [by legal proceedings] at the gate [where the city court is held]

(Proverbs 22:22-23 Amplified Bible).

This verse from Solomon's hand probably had to do with what we would call civil proceedings rather than criminal ones. The Amplified Bible gives interpretations especially where the meaning is a bit obscure —thus the words in brackets. The warning in this saying seems not to be so much to robbers contemplating their next victims as to citizens bringing lawsuits against others without any consideration of their being unlikely to be able to pay if found liable. (While in our country today we don't have "debtor's prison," the same wasn't true in Solomon's day, nor in Jesus' day.) The NIV has "exploit" for the Amplified Bible's "rob." The CEV has, "Don't take advantage of the poor or cheat them in court." This verse is about the haves targeting the have-nots, and using the courts to do it.

One might think that it wouldn't make much sense to target people who don't have money, in order to exact money. After all, as we say, You can't get blood out of a turnip.

But the have-nots are not mostly those who have absolutely nothing, but those who just have much less of it than most other people. They live paycheck to paycheck. They often have difficulty making ends meet. And it's precisely that position in the economic spectrum that makes them potential victims, not just of individuals, but of the businesses the law allows to operate, but which at their heart are infested with not only the potential to exploit the poor, but probably also the intention to do so.

I have in mind something that South Carolinians and North Carolinians, siblings among the states in some ways, have had differing laws about for some years: payday lending. Drive up the road about thirty minutes from my hometown and you won't find any payday loan business. The Tarheel State doesn't allow it. The Palmetto State does.

Probably the civil matters in which I found it the most distasteful to uphold the law over the years were those where a payday lender was suing a customer who didn't pay back a loan.

Officially known as Deferred Presentment Services, payday lending (for the reader not familiar with it) is the business of lending people money based on a paycheck they haven't received yet, with promise of payment within thirty days. It's a bit more complex than that, but that's the gist of it. In South Carolina, the lender can charge interest of 15% of the principle *per month*. As a yearly rate (APR), that would be 390%. (For comparison, most credit cards have at most a 24% APR.) Customers can have at most one loan at a time *lawfully,* but they can take out an unlimited number of loans in a year. In some states, it's still legal to take out a second payday loan to pay off a first, a third to pay off a second, and so on.

A person in South Carolina who takes out one payday loan for $550.00 in a year and pays it off on time will pay $82.50 for the privilege. A person who just can't keep up with bills (or wants) and takes out a payday loan for the maximum every month, still paying them off on time, will pay $990.00 for the service.

What makes this business an outlet for insidious evil, in my humble opinion, is that it is premised on the very fact that some people can't seem to get a handle on their bills. Their money runs out before their month, as the saying goes. The payday lending business banks on the fact that some people are always behind. Ironically, by doing business with payday lenders, these economically disadvantaged persons will become even *less* able to meet their financial obligations.

What happens, of course, is that the lenders can sue non-payers. That put them in my court. And I didn't have the option of just refusing to hear their cases. I simply could not follow the Bible's advice to *not* be an agent of exploitation. I had to uphold the law. It was the *law* that was permitting exploitation.

A lender can obtain a judgment for the amount of the unpaid loan. Based on that judgment, the lender can then record the judgment in the circuit court of the county. He can then identify property of the borrower, file an action to enforce judgment against property, and have the sheriff seize the property—a vehicle, for instance—and sell it at county auction, the proceeds paying off the loan.

But even if our example borrower pays of all his loans on time, he has still paid out nearly a thousand dollars in a year just to have his money a few weeks earlier than he would have. Where could that $990.00 have been spent last year to get what needed replacing, to fix what needed repair, to feed and clothe children, or one of a hundred other needful things. Instead, it went to line the pockets of businesses that couldn't exist without poor people to squeeze money out of.

Granted, the poor aren't dragged into these businesses against their will, except in the sense that everyone can be seduced by the promise of someone's making their lives easier. But of course, they don't do it for free. Everyone who offers to make your life better is getting a slice of your income for doing so, and in the end they may not make your life better at all.

Why our state still allows this predatory lending scheme to function legitimately is beyond me. But what keeps its corporate structure so flush with profits is poverty, pure and simple. Not the dirt poor, but the working poor.

And I couldn't do a thing about it.

Early on in my judicial career I theorized that a two-step plan could get people out of the cycle of payday loans. It was my reasonable guess than in a great majority of cases, a couple of expenditures common to each of these households were responsible for much of the depletion of family income that made payday loans necessary to make ends meet. Just two steps. Eliminate two things from the family's expenditures: beer and cigarettes.

Actually, you could probably add eating out, or one of a dozen other things, to that list of two. Probably most people's—including my own—spending habits could be inspected for some things that are wasteful. But these two items, beer and cigarettes, are probably the culprit in many lower socio-economic households. If a household would forego the beer and cigarettes for just one month, how much could they save that would put them ahead of where they were, and keep them from having to take out a payday loan the next month?

Look at a household with a husband and wife, both of whom smoke cigarettes. In South Carolina, that's not unusual at all. With an average price of a pack of cigarettes being $6.82 at this writing, assuming both husband and wife smoke a pack a day, that's $95.48 per week, or a whopping $409.20 every thirty days. We almost don't have to calculate the price of beer, but let's continue.

A case of beer in South Carolina is presently about $15.32. In some households, that case can disappear in a single weekend, but let's say that it lasts a whole week, with more than half of it being consumed on the weekend. That's $65.66 every thirty days.

By cutting out beer and cigarettes, if instead of inhaling it or drinking it this couple stuffed that money into a piggy bank, they'd have $474.86 at the end of thirty days. That might well be what they need to even their income with their expenses. If they keep it up for two months, they'll almost certainly be able to wave goodbye to the loan shark operating as a payday lender down the street. And they will likely have broken their habits of drinking and smoking, which will make them healthier.

This may seem like an elitist idea. Au contraire, mon amis, it is entirely practical. Even so, some would say it's an overly simplistic suggestion. It probably is. People's habits, wants and needs, and a thousand other things about their lives develop into intricately woven patterns that sometimes defy simple solutions to change. But then again, sometimes things are lampooned as simplistic that cannot, simply cannot be debunked. They make too much sense. Nancy Reagan, the First Lady of the United States from 1981-1989 introduced an anti-drug campaign in 1986. Its title was the core of her strategy: Just Say No. Critics laughed uproariously. They made jokes—but of course, they made jokes about both the President and his wife, and the country hasn't seen the like of them for principles, leadership, and grace in more than thirty years since. But no one has ever been able to overcome the simple logic and successful power of that strategy.

Think about it: beer and cigarettes. Just say NO.

In waking fantasies I gave a speech in court outlining this solution to people's addiction to payday lending, though in real life I never did. I couldn't see clear to justifying it in any one case, because I didn't know the particulars, and because I thought it might sound judgmental. Then again, if a judge can't sound a little bit judgmental, who can.

Turning from things a judge may not be able to control back to advice about things he *can,* the Bible recounts a trial scene where a judge did the wrong thing, and today's jurists can learn from it.

Don't Be Swayed by the Loudest Lawyer

The history of juries as finders of fact in courts goes back only a thousand years or so. Before the innovation of the jury, judgment was rendered by a single judge, or occasionally by a group of judges or a council. But most judgment was by a lone judge. Historically, those judges were not part of independent judiciaries—that's another late development in the world. In Israel they were priests. Under empires that ruled the middle east, the various political figures that were governors or prefects of the individual regions of those empires acted as judges.

So it was that Pontius Pilate took on the role of judge when he was governor of Judea. When Jesus was arrested and brought before Pilate, there was no one speaking in Jesus' defense, just Jesus himself. But the prosecution, if we can call it that, consisted of a few official Jewish leaders and apparently a substantial crowd of "witnesses," or complainants.

> "...I have examined him in your presence and have found no basis for your charges against him." ...But the whole crowd shouted, "Away with this man! Release Barabbas to us!" ...they kept shouting, "Crucify him! Crucify him!" ...with loud shouts they

insistently demanded that he be crucified, and their shouts prevailed. So Pilate decided to grant their demand (Luke 23:14-23 NIV).

This is one of the most dramatic moments in the whole of the Bible. It is most interesting that Pilate didn't find that Jesus had done anything for which he should be punished. But the loud and persistent demands of the crowd—the accusers and witnesses—swayed him.

From Matthew's gospel we have an additional detail that Pilate's wife sent a message to him *while he was on the bench,* warning him not to have anything to do with Jesus, whom she described as "an innocent man" (Matthew 27:19). She said she had had a dream about Jesus, prompting the warning.

So here is Jesus, standing before the judge, Governor Pontius Pilate, and Pilate has no evidence to convict him, and he has a solemn warning from his wife that she knows Jesus to be innocent of any wrongdoing. But he has a cadre of accusers who insist that Jesus has made claims that violate Jewish law and that merit his death. And he has a crowd of witnesses more like a mob shouting for Jesus' crucifixion. And he knows that one thing Rome dislikes just about as much as anything in their world is a riot. And he has what looks for all the world like the beginnings of a riot right in front of him. And they're shouting, louder and louder.

At this point, though Jesus answered Pilate's probing questions earlier (John 18:28-38), he becomes quiet and gives no defense to the baseless accusations of the Jewish chief priests and elders (Matthew 27:14). The sound of Pilate's court is just the ceaseless, rhythmic, loud repetition of the Jews' demands, growing in volume by the minute.

And Pilate gives in to the party that makes the most noise, even though he knew in his heart Jesus should have gone free.

In discussion of this Bible passage, someone suggested to me that Pilate was "supposed to" condemn Jesus, that if he hadn't, the plan of God for Jesus to die for the sins of humanity would not have been carried out. But the fact that everything went according to God's inscrutable eternal plan does not vindicate Pilate, anymore than God's plan to use Pharaoh to exhibit his glory in the exodus vindicated him for hardening his heart against the Hebrews, or anymore than the evil done by *anyone* in history was excused, just because their wrongdoing was worked into a plan for the divine glory by a sovereign God of miracles. Pilate made an utterly sinful judgment because he listened to the loudest, most vociferous, most demanding voice in his court that day.

Powerful spiritual lessons are in the gospels' accounts of Jesus' trial before Pilate, and I've hinted at them above. For the purposes of this book, however, we can derive this very practical piece of advice for the judge. Don't be swayed by the loudest lawyer.

Once or twice when I was on the bench I had before me two parties with attorneys, one of whom was a well known figure in the legal community of the upstate. Among other things he was known to be a ferocious advocate for his clients, "pushing the envelope," as the saying goes, in the matter of courtroom decorum and court rules, though usually without having to be reined in by a judge. But in his impassioned representation the one thing that seemed to stand out was his forceful volume. He was loud.

He was never timid sounding, never reserved. Even with his own witnesses he started questioning with an amplitude that got everyone's attention. When he was cross examining witnesses, he became louder and louder, more demanding, more forceful, and his pace usually became more rapid-fire, as he verbally worked witnesses into a corner, extracting the answers he wanted or eliciting the silence that he thought proved his point.

While many attorneys in Summary Court didn't bother with closing arguments—they saved those for the bigger stage of the circuit court—this one always closed. And the judge was not spared the loud and dramatic presentation. When arguments were finished, I had to let the ringing in my ears go away, let the reverberations in the courtroom die down, and render a verdict that was still based on the evidence and the law, not on how

111

intimidating this one particular lawyer had been in his passionate presentation for the plaintiff or his demanding defense of the defendant.

It is true that people tend to compensate for their shortcomings by emphasizing other things that draw attention away from their weaknesses. By that measure one might say that a person who is excessively loud in arguing his point may have a weak case to begin with. But the judge wouldn't want to make the mistake of assuming this to be true of a loud lawyer. If it's important not to be swayed into agreement by his volume, it's equally important not to be dissuaded from agreeing with him for the same thing. The goal is to discount the tactics used to present the case and to consider the case alone.

The judge who preceded me on the bench of my court had difficulty seeing, and somewhere in the course of his nearly four decades as a judge he became totally blind. I heard a story of how someone who didn't know he was blind came to court and presented as evidence a stack of photographs. As I heard it, the clerk who helped the judge during these hearings brought the pictures to him and fanned them out, and the judge picked them up, thumbed through them while nodding and saying, "Mmm hmm, I see," and then returned them to the clerk. If he deliberated before rendering a verdict, I think he had that clerk tell him what the pictures showed.

It wasn't an ideal situation; in fact, it was quite "iffy" as judicial procedure goes. If the party had known what was going on, there might have been basis for objection or appeal. But what happened was that the evidence was separated from its presentation. How well or how poorly the photographer had performed didn't matter. Nothing about the presentation skewed the actual evidence.

As I thought of that true and admittedly funny story about my friend, I wondered how it would be if the judge were not blind, but deaf. What if he had to read all the words of the parties and witnesses, *and their attorneys,* on a screen or even later in transcripts, and there were no loud lawyers to sway his opinion?

In reality, it's rare for a judge actually to be deaf. There is a judge in Alaska who as a lawyer became deaf and then became a judge. He has a specially trained court reporter who types 200 w.p.m. and he sees the ongoing transcript on a screen in front of him. To Judge Chuck Ray, loud lawyers are no factor at all. My research indicates there may be a hundred or more deaf judges in the United States. The rest of us have to divorce volume from content when we go to make a decision.

The number of things judges have to discount, downplay, or disregard when deciding a case is certainly longer than those I have listed in this chapter. But these and any others that may or may not have apt illustrations in the Bible exist as advice or even caveat for a good reason, which is at the core of American jurisprudence:

A Defendant is Innocent Until Proven Guilty

The judge should never let anything interrupt, foreshorten, cloud, confuse, rush, skew or do anything else that would corrupt the process of his clear thinking and sober deliberation on the facts. If he does, he potentially cheats the defendant of the guarantee that he must be *proven guilty* before having his innocence stripped from him. In America, that principle of innocence is sacrosanct.

The Bible contains an interesting story about the Apostle Paul, on his way under guard to Rome for a tribunal before Caesar. His boat was shipwrecked on the island of Malta in the Aegean Sea. Crew and passengers were making fires on the beach to get warm, and Paul put an armful of wood on the fire himself. When he did, a viper came out of the stack and latched onto his hand. Apparently with little fanfare, Paul shook the snake into the fire.

The islanders were watching the whole affair and waiting for Paul to swell up and die, and someone voiced the dire prediction, and their collective judgment, about Paul:

...They said to each other, "This man must be a

murderer; for though he escaped from the sea, the goddess Justice has not allowed him to live" (Acts 28:4 NIV).

The word "justice" in this verse is usually capitalized by translators because it is the word Diké, the name of a goddess the Greeks believed in, daughter of Themis, the Goddess of Justice. Diké was specifically believed to be the goddess who executed the just decisions and sentences of Themis (the Roman name for Themis was Justicia). The islanders who saw Paul bitten by a poisonous viper concluded automatically and instantly that he was guilty of murder or something else worthy of death, and they thought surely he would shortly drop dead. The story goes on to say that when he didn't, they concluded exactly the opposite, that he was a god.

Here on display, then, is a conclusion of guilt without adequate evidence to convict. In addition to the spiritual lessons the Christian might derive from this account, the moral of the story for purposes of this book is never to assume that if someone has been charged, he *must* be guilty; that if he's in court, he must have done *something* wrong.

The principle of a Summary Court is found in the definition of that word "summary." Merriam-Webster says it means, "done without delay or formality: quickly executed." To the average reader or viewer of the news it seems that after crimes are committed, people are slow to be charged, slow to be tried, slow to be acquitted or convicted, slow to be sentenced if guilty, and slow for sentence to be carried out on them. By contrast, the Summary Court exists to take care of legal matters promptly, when charges are relatively minor.

Sometimes, however, especially in criminal matters, the expected pace of justice in Summary Courts may induce in a judge a tendency, if not exactly to move things along quickly, then at least not to take all the time he *needs*, to make certain that a defendant's rights are fully granted, the evidence against him is thoroughly weighed, and the evidence in his favor is completely considered. If "summary" winds up meaning "rushed," then the presumption of innocence is in jeopardy.

While we have been able to glean principles and advice for judges irrespective of whether they are Bible-believing persons, some words of wisdom and inspiration the Bible offers for the sober consideration of jurists is specifically directed toward those who *do* believe the word of God and who *are* numbered among his people. To these people the scripture's inspiring word is about an awesome responsibility the godly judge has. To that duty we now turn.

Judging for the Lord

In my early morning Bible reading and time of spiritual devotion, for some years I have read through the Old Testament every six months and the New Testament at the same time, every two months. Consequently I have read 2 Chronicles 19:5-6 twice a year. But not until I became a judge did these verses jump off the page and strike me in a profound way.

> [Jehoshaphat] appointed judges in the land, in each of the fortified cities of Judah. He told them, "Consider carefully what you do, because you are not judging for mere mortals but for the Lord, who is with you whenever you give a verdict" (2 Chronicles 19:5-6 NIV).

Compare this translation to some of the other offerings available, particularly of v.6:

> ...Always think carefully before pronouncing judgment. Remember that you do not judge to please people but to please the LORD (NLT).

The NLT takes the Hebrew to mean "to please the Lord," where the King James and most other versions stay closer to the literal rendering, which means "on behalf of the Lord." But the NLT, as a mostly paraphrase translation, tries to get at conversational meaning.

> **...Consider what you are doing, for you do not judge for mankind but for the LORD who is with you when you render judgment (NASB).**

The New American Standard Bible takes "man" to mean "mankind," emphasizing the judge as he relates to the entire, ongoing race of humankind. But note:

> **...Consider what you are doing, for you do not judge for a man, but for the LORD, who is with you in the matter of judgment (CSB).**

The (Holman) Christian Standard Bible takes the opposite view, that the Hebrew *le'adam* implies the indefinite article, thus, "a man." This emphasizes the individual human being, the particular case the judge is hearing.

The Contemporary English Version has a very different take on v.6:

> **...Be careful when you make your decisions in court, because you are judging by the LORD's standards and not by human standards, and he will know what you decide (CEV).**

The CEV very loosely makes an interpretational leap in this verse. The translators assumed Jehoshaphat was charging his judges to stick to the word of God in their judgments and not to accept other ideas that have no basis in God's word. Doubtless, this would have been good advice for priest-judges, but it isn't really an accurate rendering of the original language.

The Good News Translation, which we have used before in this book, goes a little far afield from the original Hebrew as well:

...Be careful in pronouncing judgment; you are not acting on human authority, but on the authority of the LORD, and he is with you when you pass sentence (GNT).

The New American Bible (a Roman Catholic approved Bible), goes even further in its exaltation of the judge's ultimate authority:

...Take care what you do, for the judgment you give is not human but divine; for when it comes to judgment God will be with you (NAB).

Obviously translators have tried to pinpoint the meaning and have come at the words from slightly different perspectives. But the bottom line is that Jehoshaphat told his judges that they were not performing a merely secular task but a divinely instituted one, and that they were to have an attitude about what they were doing that it was "the Lord's work," as we sometimes say today. Consequently, they could expect that if they were careful to approach their task spiritually, prayerfully, and out of a life of faithfulness to God, he would bless their work and even inhabit their judgments in such a way that people would recognize divine inspiration in what they did.

On one of my complete readings through the Old Testament, I remember when I first read 2 Chronicles 19:5-6 as a judge. Two things instantly came across to my heart.

One was that I saw more completely than ever before the connection between the profession I had moved into with the profession I had pursued the first quarter century of my adult life. I had not been troubled about moving out of full time pastoral work into full time judicial work. But subconsciously I had been looking for the divine connection between the two: a life of Bible teaching and spiritual leadership, and a life of rendering justice in a court.

Here was that connection. Since, in ancient Israel, priests served as judges, it is highly reasonable to assume that Jehoshaphat's appointments of judges were within the priestly class. In the same way that some of Jehoshaphat's priests handled the tasks of the temple and some of them handled the calling of the courtroom, so I was now moving from the pulpit to the bench. And the word of God was reminding me that I was still doing "the Lord's work."

This minor epiphany didn't relieve me of any future obligation to preach the word of God. It just gave me a deeper, scripturally based understanding of the divine hand in the pilgrimage of my years. My brother, who had been my closest friend and counselor through my struggling years in difficult pastorates, upon hearing of my opportunity to become a judge had one word: "Perfect!"

The second thing that happened to me when I "discovered" 2 Chronicles 9:5-6 in a personal way was that I was hit with a wave of inspiration. I had taken on the judicial role with high enthusiasm and a conviction that it was right for me, at just the right time. But an even greater inspiration came over me as I found my calling to this particular role within the Lord's will. I saw myself in those two verses of scripture. I wrote in my Bible beside them, "And THIS explains how I can be a Preacher AND a Judge."

Obviously, this Bible passage was not written only for me. It has application to every Christian judge. Two challenges emerge from Jehoshaphat's charge to his judges:

Regard Your Role as a High, Holy Task

Every judge who holds to the Christian faith should look at his profession as an opportunity to serve God. It is a holy task.

You are not judging for mere mortals but for the LORD

119

(2 Chronicles 19:6 NIV).

Arguably, every profession, even every mundane job, that a Christian pursues should be looked at—in the very least—as an opportunity to serve God's purposes. The Apostle Paul argued this point effectively in 1 Corinthians 10:31 when he expanded from a little debate about scruples over food to a much larger, spiritual principle: "Do *all* to the glory of God" (ESV, emphasis mine).

The Old Testament contained this same challenge. Solomon wrote in Ecclesiastes 9:10, "Whatever your hand finds to do, do it with all your might." God wants us to have enthusiasm in our work.

It has often been pointed out that our English word "enthusiasm" comes from *enthousiasmos*, Greek for "inspiration or possession by God (or "a" god). The word came into English sometime in the 1600s and at first was used in this original sense, to express religious fervor. A hundred years or so later it took on the more general sense it has today. But whenever you read 1 Corinthians 10:31 or Ecclesiastes 9:10, add the word "enthusiastically!" and remember where it comes from.

Being a judge is a holy task, in the view of scripture. In the judge's determination of guilt or innocence (or "not guilty") he is expected by the public to speak as if God were speaking and to render true justice.

The case against a defendant may be as clear as a bell and not beyond real question of fact. Still, the defendant may exercise his Constitutional right and plead "not guilty," which is a demand for the State to prove its case beyond reasonable doubt. That standard, "beyond reasonable doubt," is not the same as "beyond the shadow of doubt," or "beyond all doubt," but the public may have absolutely *no* doubt of the defendant's guilt and, in these days of ubiquitous video cameras, there may be a crystal clear video of the defendant doing what he is charged with. Still, the matter is in court, and a verdict of guilty or not guilty must still be rendered.

A jury may have been empaneled to render this verdict, of course, and the high, holy task shifts to them. I admit to some feelings of relief when a jury would be rendering judgment in my place in some specific circumstance, but even when they did, sentencing was my purview.

But for the sake of the historical image consider the judge alone, in the moment of judgment. It is no small thing he does, and he shouldn't think of it as a job that just anyone can do. Nor is it a role he was given merely because of his interest in it or education for it. The men and women of government who were involved in his being on the bench had something to do with it. The voters were involved if he was elected. The senators were involved if he was nominated. The governor was involved if he was appointed. But if he's a Christian and he's a judge, no matter who else's hand was in it, he serves because God's hand was above them all. That makes the bench a high, holy task.

The second challenge for today's Christian judge from ancient Jehoshaphat's instructions to his judges is equally inspirational:

Be Confident of God's Presence When You Sentence

Jehoshaphat's charge to his judges was abundantly clear:

The Lord ...is with you whenever you give a verdict (2 Chronicles 19:6 NIV).

or as the GNT puts it:

...he is with you when you pass sentence.

The Hebrew word *mispat,* which we earlier described as meaning "judgment," pictures the judge delivering his verdict, which would include sentencing. At least one version, however, has, "when you hear a case." All the translations are trying to communicate the sense of the verse in the idiom of modern circumstances.

But there's an element to this verse that I haven't yet discussed. It's the implied, or semi-expressed, condition of the promise of the Lord's presence.

The verse begins with the words, "Consider carefully what you do" (2 Chronicles 19:6a). The first word, "Consider," is the often-found word *rəu,* which is often translated simply, "see" or "take heed." Other translations of this verse have, "Pay attention," "Be careful," or "Think carefully." It could also be translated, "Be mindful." Why would that word of caution precede the promise that the Lord will be with the judge when he judges?

The reason can't be simply that the judge shouldn't fail to be aware of God's presence in his judgment, as if somehow, if he weren't, he would involve God in a mistaken verdict. That interpretation would not comport with what we know of God.

Rather, what we have here is an implied condition of God's blessing on the judge's work: the judge will do his work—hear complaints, consider evidence, deliberate with wisdom, render a verdict, and pass sentence or issue orders—with the full authority of the Lord himself, *as, and when, he lives and works in a daily mindfulness of God's holy presence.*

The judge who regards his life as a pilgrimage upon which God has led him, and sees his position as judge as one to which God directed him, and sees his task as holy, may be absolutely confident that as he carries out his duties faithfully, God is with him: God is behind him in support; God is with him in fellowship; God is in front of him in whatever may eventuate because of his rulings; God is around him in protection; God is within him inspiring him to speak. The judge's verdict is a high point in the performance of his duties, and God has surrounded him for the inspiration, certainty and strength he needs.

Humanity being what it is, of course, people who are Christians and judges can, and do, make mistakes. Wrong decisions result from any number of wrong thoughts, wrong conclusions, failure to eliminate prejudices, or just failure to be walking closely with God throughout one's day or at a period of one's life.

But this promise given by Jehoshaphat to his judges was something like what the Apostle Paul promised Christians in Galatians 5:16: "Walk by the Spirit, and you will not gratify the desires of the flesh." That is an amazing, blanket promise of God's word that the believer in Christ who keeps up a perfect fellowship with him through the Holy Spirit will not sin!

Earlier in life, during my pastoral ministry career, I preached on this teaching of Paul's, and a deacon took issue with me. He said I was saying Christians could live perfect lives. That's not what I said, of course. I merely explained what Paul very simply said. And the promise, "not gratify," was based on the condition, "Walk by the Spirit."

I should have told the deacon what preacher Bailey Smith once said in a Southern Baptist Convention meeting. He was preaching and was focusing on a very powerful Bible truth. Someone in the vast crowd in the arena shouted out, heckling him. Smith looked in the direction of the heckler, pointed his finger and said, "Don't argue with me, sir: argue with the Bible, and then repent!"

The promise given in 2 Chronicles 19:6 is not vague, not a wish, and not a generalization. It is conditioned on the godly living of the judge. But given the fulfillment of that condition, it is a firm promise that the godly man or woman who serves as a judge may be certain that *if* he is living in full harmony with the Lord and relying on his Spirit for guidance, the Lord *will* be with him when he renders judgment.

The fly in the ointment, of course, is that we get distracted, we make little, wrong choices, we do *something, anything wrong,* and the perfect fellowship with the Spirit becomes temporarily imperfect and even more mistakes (or worse) can happen.

The same is true of the promise to judges. It should be taken as a lofty principle to be strived for every day, throughout the course of the judge's time on the bench. Like every goal of life, it is as certain as heaven but unseen from earth.

But this promise is at work in the Christian judge uniquely. It gives him an edge on the judge who has yet to meet and know the

Judge of all the earth.

I'll allow a restatement of 2 Chronicles 19:5-6 to make the closing argument for the reader-judge's consideration:

The judge is to take the position that while he is a human being and he is making a decision between human beings (or between the government of human beings and individual citizen human beings), nevertheless in the greater sense he is the representative of the Lord, rendering judgment in matters of law and equity for God. In other words, if the litigants or defendants were to have had the privilege of having God *himself* as their judge, the outcome would not have differed. This profound understanding of the judge's role is meant to humble him and focus him on the highest standard of justice.

Court is Adjourned

It was my goal in *The Bible & The Bench* to inspire other judges to follow God's principles, wisdom, and advice for their judicial role and to take God up on his promise to make them equal to their holy task. I hope I have done that.

First and foremost, God is the ultimate source of justice, and the system in any nation is most just when it recognizes the justice of the God of the Bible and follows his principles. Within such a system, individual judges serve the people as the representatives of God among them.

Because the judge is God's representative, he must model personal righteousness, since without his being, himself, just, he cannot ultimately render justice to others. He must be fair and impartial, beyond all kinds of corruption, and must excel in wisdom.

People will notice that kind of wisdom. It will exhibit itself in the judge's contemplative demeanor, his measured sentencing, his exhibition of mercy where needed, and his even-handed dealings with even those whose behavior invites contempt. The judge will show his or her wisdom by detecting and avoiding exploitation, by letting the clearest facts determine a case instead of the most seductive speaker, and by always treating those charged as innocent until the last word is in and they are either guilty or not.

Finally, the judge who is not just an intellectual student of the principles of justice contained in the Bible, but also a personal follower of Jesus Christ—the Word of God made flesh (John 1:14), the wisdom of God (1 Corinthians 1:24), and ultimate judge (2 Corinthians 5:10)—will recognize that his or hers is one of the more sacred roles that human beings can perform on this side of heaven. Accordingly, the Christian judge will take on his task out of a life of faithful discipleship to Jesus Christ and with the presence and fulness of the Holy Spirit when he renders justice to people before him.

In looking back on my experience as a judge, I would not dare to say that I performed perfectly in all respects. Most of us, if summing up only a single *day* of our lives, would have to admit that most days were spattered with blotches of sinfulness, however minor, involving words spoken, things done, and things left undone. Knowing this, we should be disinclined to think for even a moment that *years* have gone by without one spot of disobedience, one moment of unfaithfulness, or one hour of unworthiness. I don't make any such claim about my life or about my judicial work.

However, I can say and I will say that as I look back on my years on the bench, I find it remarkable but equally as true that I do not regret one decision I made, in any case, criminal or civil. I have no doubt that many people whose opponents prevailed in court thought I had made a mistake. I have no doubt that a few of those charged with crimes didn't *like* my judgments against them. But I cannot think of a single decision I rendered that I later believed I had gotten wrong.

In civil cases, I was appealed to the higher court only a dozen or so times over the years, and I was upheld every time but once. Even in that case, the basis of appeal was a technicality, and when the case was retried by another judge—at my request—he rendered the same verdict.

By the grace of God, I arrived at the day of my retirement without a single misgiving about any judgment lingering in my mind to cause regret. And for that, I give the Lord my most humble thanks.

Abbreviations of Translations Used

AMP	Amplified Bible
ASV	American Standard Version
BSB	Berean Study Bible
CEV	Contemporary English Version
CSB	Christian Standard Bible
ERV	English Revised Version
ESV	English Standard Version
GNT	Good News Translation
GWT	God's Word® Translation
HCSB	Holman Christian Standard Bible
ISV	International Standard Version
KJV	King James Version
NAS	New American Standard
NIV	New International Version
NKJ	New King James Version
NLT	New Living Translation

www.ingramcontent.com/pod-product-compliance
Lightning Source LLC
Chambersburg PA
CBHW030731150426
42813CB00051B/414